TANTE HEIDI'S SWISS KITCHEN

TANTE HEIDI'S

Swiss Kitchen

BY EVA MARIA BORER

TRANSLATED BY HILDA MORRIS

AND ADAPTED BY SHEILA WATSON

WITH LINE DRAWINGS BY
JUDITH OLONETZKY-BALTENSPERGER

GRAMERCY PUBLISHING COMPANY • NEW YORK

Library of Congress Catalog Card Number: 66-24657

This edition published by Gramercy Publishing Company
a division of Crown Publishers, Inc.
by arrangement with A. S. Barnes and Co., Inc.
a b c d e f g h

Printed in the United States of America

CONTENTS

Introduction, vii
Useful Facts and Figures, x
Oven Temperature Chart, xii

Satisfying Soups, 1
Cheese Specialities, 10
Fish for the Gourmet, 23
Meat and Poultry Dishes, 32
Popular Sausage Dishes, 48
Potatoes Cooked in Many Ways, 52
Pasta, Rice, Dumplings and Cereals, 60
Bread . . . with Butter, Eggs and Milk, 68
Sweet and Savoury Tarts and Pasties, 75
Desserts, 83
Out of the Frying Pan, 87
Cakes, Pastries and Biscuits, 93
A Note on Drinks, 110
A Feast from the Good Old Days, 111
Modern Health Cookery, 114
- The Modern Swiss Kitchen, 115
- Fruit and Vegetable Juices, 116
- Salads, 117
- Presenting Raw Vegetables, 120
- Swiss Muesli, 121
- Fruit Dishes, 123
- Vegetable Cookery, 124

Appendixes:
- A Little List of Swiss Sausages, 135
- Different Swiss Breads, 136

Bibliography, 138
Index of English Names, 139
Index of Swiss Names, 145

INTRODUCTION

Some may say there is no such thing as the 'Swiss kitchen' and never has been, either in the past when every mountain valley was a world of its own, or today—for on the gastronomic map of Switzerland there is no capital. Cookery lore comes in four different languages and regional specialities are jealously guarded secrets: the famous fried potatoes are 'Bernese Rösti', the flour soup is 'Basle Flour Soup', fondue is Fondue Neuchâtel or Fondue Fribourg, and so the list goes on. So when we talk about Swiss food, we refer mainly to these specialities of the different cantons and districts, of which there are so many in Switzerland, and which enable Swiss menus to ring numerous changes and offer delicious surprises. The foreign holiday guest, of course, will be introduced to only a few of them, since most of the international hotels follow the classical French cuisine. But most who return from Switzerland treasure the memory of at least one of the memorable national dishes, now, alas, rapidly vanishing from private homes and even the farmer's kitchen, but often both original *and* simple to prepare, and well worth preserving.

The most important contributions come from the Emmenthal with its cheese, its fried potatoes and yeast plaits, and its famous piggeries to which we owe the juicy peasant ham and the 'Bernese Board'. The inner Swiss cantons offer a great variety of simple, tasty dishes prepared with milk, butter, cream and cheese—you can almost hear the sound of cow bells. The cuisine of western Switzerland shows a strong French influence. From this region come the wines produced on the shores of Lake Geneva and Lake Neuchâtel, and the slopes of Wallis, as well as some of the most delicious cheese dishes, among them 'fondue', that bold and famous combination of cheese with white wine. Eastern Switzerland is known for its sausages, its pale-red country wine, its 'Wähen' and other pastries. Graubünden is a culinary realm of its own: from earliest times, many strange ingredients from Austria and the Balkan regions were imported over its mountain passes, among them maize (locally still called 'Turkish corn'), and modified according to the taste of the mountain people. From Graubünden hails the delicious air-dried Bündner meat, which is cut in diaphanous slices and eaten with pepper, as well as perhaps the best tarts and pastries of all kinds. The fame of the sweets created by adventurous pastrycooks, or 'sugar bakers', of the Engadine has carried over the world. The inhabitants of the Tessin, whose cooking is closely related to that of northern Italy, have taught their fellow countrymen on the north side of the St Gotthard Pass how properly to prepare and enjoy rice, maize and spaghetti. Finally, the bigger cities like Zürich, Geneva, Berne, Basle, Lucerne and St Gallen have their own specialities, among them some remarkable ways of preparing meat and fish and, last but not least, their sweets and special pastries.

In this book I have incorporated as representative a selection as possible from the wide variety of recipes which have been evolved over the years in the twenty-two Swiss cantons. I have not attempted an exhaustive list—that would obviously be impossible, since many similar dishes are prepared slightly differently from canton to canton, from valley to valley, and also bear different names in different districts. Dishes which in their original form were too rich and indigestible have been adapted to suit modern standards, or I have chosen from several methods of preparation that which best meets our needs. In some cases it has been a matter of trial and error, for in the old cookery books and handwritten notes which have served as sources there are rarely any indications of weights and measures! In the old days, rule of thumb served in place of kitchen scales.

Dishes from neighbouring countries have not been included, even though they may have been adopted by the Swiss, unless a truly Swiss form exists. Otherwise I should not have known where to begin and where to end. Anywhere in Switzerland today you can enjoy not only *pommes frites*, and excellent grills, not only Italian spaghetti, Risotto and pizza, but specialities from Spain, or lands of the Far East, as well. That, too, is a feature of the modern Swiss kitchen.

One aspect I could not omit is that regarded by many people abroad as the only 'real' Swiss kitchen: the modern 'reform' cooking which from its inception has been closely connected with the name of Dr Bircher. At the turn of the century, long before similar movements were established elsewhere, many Swiss housewives were already making a feature of raw vegetables, Bircher Muesli and wholemeal bread, and avoiding highly refined foodstuffs. The second and shorter section of this book: 'Switzerland and Modern Health Cookery', is therefore devoted to the essential principles of this movement, a selection of delicious recipes for salads and uncooked dishes, and the modern preparation of vegetables and fruit dishes.

And now you are invited to make the culinary tour of Switzerland through the centuries to the present day, to sample soups and stews, fondue and Raclette and cheese dishes galore, Rösti and Wähen and sweets and pastries. Wherever we go, people will wish us '*En Guete !*'—'*Bon Appétit*'.

EVA MARIA BORER

USEFUL FACTS AND FIGURES

Weights and Measures

English weights and measures have been used throughout this book. In case it is wished to translate these into their American counterparts, the following tables give an approximate comparison.

Liquid Measures

1 U.S. pint = 16 fl. oz.

1 British pint = 20 fl. oz.

2 American measuring cups may be regarded for all practical purposes as equal to 1 U.S. pint of liquid. American cups are standard '½-pint' measuring cups, equal to two-fifths of a British pint. ½ American cup is equal to 6½ British tablespoons. 1 British tablespoon equals 3 teaspoons.

Average British teacup = ¼ pint = 5 fl. oz.

Average British breakfast cup = ½ pint = 10 fl. oz.

Solid Measures (approximate equivalents)

SPOONS

	BRITISH MEASURES	AMERICAN MEASURES
1 oz. sugar	1 rounded tablespoon (castor)	3 level tablespoons (granulated)
1 oz. icing or confectioner's sugar	1 heaped tablespoon	4 level tablespoons
1 oz. flour	1 heaped tablespoon	4 level tablespoons
1 oz. soft bread-crumbs	3 heaped tablespoons	8 level tablespoons
1 oz. grated cheese	2 heaped tablespoons	5 level tablespoons

AMERICAN STANDARD CUPS

1 cup syrup/treacle = 11 oz.
1 cup sugar = 8 oz.
1 cup confectioner's sugar = 6 oz.
1 cup olive oil = 8 fl. oz.
1 cup butter, margarine or lard = 8 oz.
1 cup shortening (whipped cooking fat) = 5 oz.
1 cup grated cheese = 3 oz.
1 cup breadcrumbs = 2½ oz.
1 cup rice = 7 oz.
1 cup flour = 4½ oz.
1 cup raisins = 6 oz.
1 cup currants = 6 oz.
1 cup almonds = 5 oz.

Metric Weights and Measures

It is difficult to convert to metric measures with absolute accuracy, but 1 oz. is equal to approximately 30 grammes, 2 lb. 3 oz. to 1 kilogramme. For liquid measures, approximately 1¾ English pints may be regarded as equal to 1 litre; 1 demilitre is a generous English ¾ pint, and one decilitre is 3–4 fl. oz.

Comparative Products

English castor sugar equals American granulated sugar. Icing sugar is equivalent to the American confectioner's sugar. American powdered sugar comes somewhere between the two.

Where baking powder is indicated, two-thirds the amount of American baking powder should be used, as American baking powder is stronger.

Plain flour has been used throughout unless otherwise specified. The measure indicates weight of unsifted flour.

Single (light) cream, and not double (heavy) cream has been used.

All quantities are for 4 unless otherwise stated.

Oven Temperatures

HEAT OF OVEN	GAS MARK	APPROXIMATE TEMPERATURE IN CENTRE OF OVEN (°F.)
VERY COOL	¼	240
	½	265
	1	290
COOL	2	310
WARM	3	335
MODERATE	4	355
FAIRLY HOT	5	380
	6	400
HOT	7	425
VERY HOT	8	445
	9	470

Note: This table is an approximate guide only. Different makes of cooker vary and if you are in any doubt about the setting, it is as well to refer to the manufacturer's temperature chart.

SATISFYING SOUPS

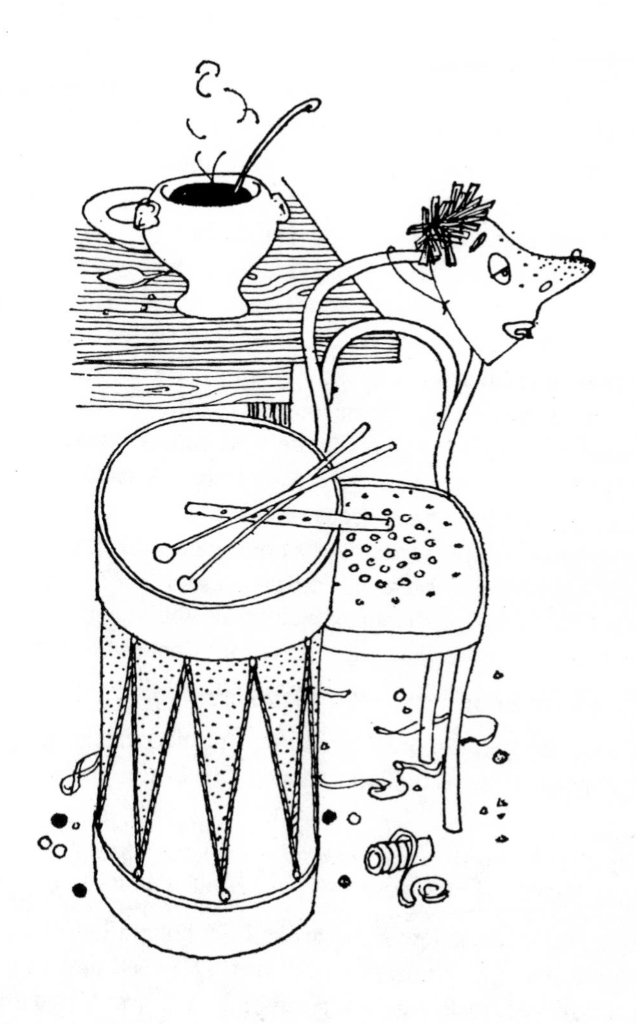

Basle Carnival

No Swiss has ever refused his soup! Soups continue to be highly regarded throughout Switzerland, even if not the soups of the 'good old days', which were cooked for two or three hours over a wood fire. The 'Swiss soups' which have gained world fame in recent years are factory-produced and can be easily prepared in five to ten minutes. They are not only convenient to use but cheap and tasty and have penetrated to the furthest mountain village: though the equivalent of the French *pot-au-feu* is still widely popular and made in homes and restaurants (p. 33).

Otherwise this chapter on soups amounts mainly to an historical survey. In peasant cookery, soups used to be dishes in which smoked or fresh meat was both cooked and served together with the other ingredients. A speciality in the 'cheese country' of Switzerland were the cheese soups of the different cantons (included in the chapter on Cheese Specialities): thick broths of bread and cheese to which were added onions, fried in butter—a mixture to horrify anyone accustomed to counting calories! The most original soups were, and sometimes still are, served in Graubünden; they above all others deserve to be saved from oblivion.

Basle Flour Soup *Basler Mehlsuppe*

This soup is eaten not only for dinner but often in the early hours after a party and particularly during the Basle Carnival.

$2\frac{1}{2}$ oz. butter
$2\frac{1}{2}$ pints beef stock (made with stock cubes if necessary)
$3\frac{3}{4}$ oz. flour
2 oz. grated cheese + extra for handing round

Heat butter in a shallow iron pan and fry flour till golden brown, stirring constantly. Work in $\frac{1}{4}$ pint stock. Pour all into a saucepan and add rest of stock. Allow to simmer on low heat for 30 minutes. Pass through a sieve, add grated cheese. Serve with additional grated cheese, so that everyone can help themselves.

Under the name of 'Guarn', a similar brown flour soup is made in Graubünden which, however, is prepared not with stock but with salted water. Two tablespoons red wine and 1 teaspoon sugar per plate are added to give the soup its special flavour.

Bread Soup and Pancake Soup

Dünkli Suppe und Flädli Suppe

The most popular soup ingredients are pancakes and bread. 'Dünkli' are thin slices of white bread, dried out on a baking sheet in the oven and stored in tins—a good way of using up stale bread. 'Flädli', too, can be made from left-overs: a pancake or two, rolled and cut into thin strips. Both are added to hot stock, together with chopped parsley and chives.

Stuffed Lettuce Soup *Gefüllte Kopfsalatsuppe*
[Graubünden]

A soup for the gourmet, said to originate at Chur.

fat for frying
heads of 6 lettuce
9 oz. veal
½ calf's brain
marjoram, salt, pepper
2 eggs
3¾ oz. white bread soaked in water
1 oz. grated Parmesan cheese
2½ pints stock
toast or cubes of fried bread
grated cheese

Carefully wash lettuce in salt water, rinse, pour over boiling water. Cut veal in pieces and fry, then add brain and fry; chop, and add marjoram, salt, pepper and 2 whole eggs. Mix well and stir in soaked bread and 2 dessertspoons Parmesan cheese. Two tablespoons of this mixture are placed in the middle of each lettuce and the leaves carefully twisted together to keep the stuffing in place (or tie with a little thin string). Gently lower stuffed lettuce into the boiling stock and allow to simmer for 15 minutes. Serve with toast and grated cheese.

Maize Soup *Maissuppe*
[Graubünden]

In Graubünden maize or Indian corn is variously known as

'Polenta flour', 'Turkish flour', and 'Saracen flour'. It is fine-ground and used in the preparation of a variety of dishes, a number of which are included in this book.

This recipe should use maize semolina, but if not available use the ordinary semolina we all know.

2½ fl. oz. milk
3¾ oz. semolina
2½ pints stock or salted water
grated Parmesan cheese

Pour milk over semolina and leave to swell for 10 minutes. Pour into the boiling stock or salted water and allow to boil for 30 minutes, stirring occasionally. Finally add grated Parmesan cheese.

Engadine Barley Soup *Engadiner Gerstensuppe*

[Graubünden]

This dish is intended for the cold weather, preferably after hard physical work! It can be made less rich and will still be tasty and nourishing.

8 oz. ham or smoked tongue
8 oz. stewing beef
5½ oz. barley
2 oz. haricot beans
8 oz. diced potatoes
1 small cabbage
3 tablespoons cream
1 oz. flour

Bring ham, beef, barley and beans to boil in about 2½ pints water and allow to simmer for about 2 hours. Add shredded cabbage and potatoes (other vegetables such as carrots and celery can be added if desired). After a further hour's cooking, thicken soup with cream previously blended with the flour, bring to the boil once more, and serve.

Pea Soup with Gnagi *Erbssuppe mit Gnagi*

[Canton Bern]

To every Swiss male, 'Gnagi' is a word to conjure with. 'Gnagi' are the coarser parts of the pig which lend themselves to 'gnawing': the forelegs, trotters, ears and tongue. Cured in brine they are often eaten as a snack before dinner, the connoisseur making his choice from a selection of Gnagi placed before him. The head of the family, who would normally scorn to do shopping of any kind, will frequently make an exception and bring home some 'Gnagi'. They are best in the canton of Bern, which is famous for pig-breeding, and Pea Soup with 'Gnagi' makes a meal on its own.

1 pair pig's trotters, cured in brine
3½–4 pints water
8 oz. dried peas
1 onion
2 oz. butter
bread cubes

Wash trotters, add cold water and parboil for about 1 hour. Add peas (which should be soaked the night before) and cook until tender, about 1½ hours. Fry chopped onion and bread cubes in butter till light brown, add to the soup, and serve.

Pot Soup with Amplis *Hafensuppe mit Amplis*
[Graubünden]

A Graubünden cookery book published in 1905 lists this soup under the name of 'Graubünden Sunday Soup'—if you eat it on Sunday, you probably won't need to think about food again for several days!

Smoked beef (ordinary beef does equally well), sausages, herbs, barley and haricot beans (you choose your own quantities) are boiled together in water in a large saucepan. One hour before the meal, pork and 'Amplis' are added.

Amplis are large dumplings and are a speciality of Graubünden farms. Mix 1 part semolina, 2 parts flour, salt, small grapes or chopped pears, together with ample lard and milk, into a thick paste. Form paste into dumplings each the size of a fist. Place each dumpling in a small linen or muslin bag to prevent crumbling and boil for 1 hour with the meat, etc.

Spinach Soup *Spinatsuppe*
[Aargau]

1 tablespoon butter or fat
4 oz. diced bacon
salt
pepper

2–3 onions, chopped
1 oz. flour
2½ fl. oz. milk
2½ pints stock
8 oz. spinach
nutmeg (if desired)
2 tablespoons cream
toast cubes
grated cheese

Fry bacon and onions until tender but not brown, add flour and stir in milk. Add beef stock (which can be made with stock cubes), bring to boil and add the well-washed, coarsely chopped spinach and seasonings. Boil for 12 minutes only! The soup may be passed through a fine sieve or not, as desired, and is improved by the addition of a few spoonfuls of cream before serving with toast and grated cheese. The same soup can be made with left-over cooked spinach. If spinach is young and tender, keep back a handful and add it, chopped, to the finished soup.

Country Soup *Zuppa del paes*

[Tessin]

In Italy a similar soup is called *Zuppa alla Pavese* and the resemblance in name suggests that the Swiss one, which means 'country soup', is a corruption of the Italian.

Per person:

1 large or 2 small slices bread
2 oz. butter
1 egg
10 fl. oz. beef stock
grated cheese
1 teaspoon tomato purée (optional)

If you wish to serve the soup as they do in Tessin, you need a small fireproof dish for each person, which can be brought straight from the cooker to table. Fry bread slices in butter and place one or two in each dish; break in an egg and, if liked, add 1 teaspoon tomato purée. Top up with boiling stock and heat for a few moments. The egg white should be just starting to thicken as you serve the soup—dishes will be very hot!—and hand the grated Parmesan cheese separately.

Cabbage Soup *Kohlsuppe*
[Canton Schwyz]

1 small cabbage
1 onion
1½ oz. butter or fat
2½ pints beef stock
2 oz. rice
salt
pepper
nutmeg
grated cheese

Gently cook the washed, shredded cabbage and chopped onion in butter until tender, turn into saucepan and pour on the stock. Allow to boil for 15 minutes, add rice and seasonings, and keep boiling until rice is soft. Cover bottom of soup tureen with grated cheese and pour in the soup, placing an extra dish of grated cheese on the table.

Minestrone *Minestrone*
[Tessin]

On both sides of the St Gotthard Pass this tasty soup is greatly esteemed, and that of the Tessin is very similar to the Italian Minestrone.

14 oz. French beans
10 oz. cabbage
10 oz. carrots
10 oz. vegetable marrow
2–3 leeks
1 head celery
2 oz. bacon
2 oz. butter
1 onion
sprig of sage
sprig of parsley
1 small tin tomato purée
salt, pepper
meat extract or cubes (optional)
2 pork sausages (optional)
8 oz. rice or spaghetti
1 lb. potatoes
grated Parmesan cheese

Place all washed, diced vegetables except onion and potatoes in boiling water. Fry chopped bacon in butter, with chopped onion and little sage. Add bacon, onion, etc., to vegetables in soup, together with parsley, pork sausages and meat extract, etc. (if used), tomato purée and seasonings. Cook for 3 hours. Add rice or spaghetti and diced potatoes 25 minutes before serving. Serve grated cheese separately.

Vegetable Marrow Soup *Kürbissuppe*
[Tessin]

One of the little-known soups.

1 large vegetable marrow	1 oz. butter
2½ pints meat or vegetable stock	toast cubes
good ½ pint milk	grated cheese
1 oz. flour	

Peel marrow, and scoop out and discard seeds; dice and cook marrow in salted water until soft. Pour off water and pass marrow through sieve, add stock. Stir soup until it comes to the boil. Stir milk into flour until smooth, add to soup and allow to boil for a further 25 minutes. Finally add knob of butter. Serve with toast cubes and grated cheese.

Tripe Soup *Busecca Kuttelsuppe*
[Tessin]

With soups, it is difficult to state the precise weights and amounts of all ingredients: the good cook takes what she finds in the kitchen and, like a chef, tastes for flavour. The preparation of this Tripe Soup follows the description of the Swiss artist Jacob Flach and is taken from his book *Minestra*, published in 1937. 'Crumble fresh rolls, drink down the thick Nostrano [red wine grown in the Tessin] and eat the Busecca in silence.

'That is a Tessin dish and a whole meal at the same time. On market days, farmers come from the valleys to Locarno to buy a cow, sell some pigs, vegetables, cheese. At lunch-time they enter one of the inns which bears, chalked up, the message "*Oggi Busecca*" (tripe soup today). Seen through the kitchen door, here's what happens:

'Greenstuff of all kinds, cabbage, celery, leeks, are cleaned and shredded, carrots are grated, and everything is fried in oil. Hot water or stock is poured in, then the cooking continues in an open pan. Plenty of well-cleaned tripe (it must be well cleaned to give the proper taste), not too fat and cut in narrow strips, is parboiled in salted water, with a teaspoon of caraway seeds, a glass of white wine and a handful of pasta, which in this part of the country are called by such pious names as Ave Maria, Paternoster, and so on, according to shape. The mixture is boiled until tender and served with grated Sbrinz cheese.'

CHEESE SPECIALITIES

Heidi and Her Grandfather

There is no other country in the world which can offer so many different kinds of regional cheese dishes in so small a space as Switzerland. Some of them, like fondue, have gained world-wide fame; others are widely popular throughout Switzerland, as are the different cheese fritters; and some, equally delicious, like the Appenzell Cheese Balls, are known only in their particular corner of the country. The following recipes offer a selection.

A WORD ABOUT SWISS CHEESES

Switzerland produces some hundred different kinds of cheese. The most famous is Emmenthal with its large holes, sometimes known, particularly in America, simply as 'Swiss cheese'. Somewhat similar, but lighter in colour and of a special piquancy, is Greyerzer, which is made chiefly in the west of the country and there called Gruyère. Tilsit and Sbrinz are other cheeses which can be had anywhere in Switzerland. In the recipes I have given, as far as possible, the names of the original cheeses with which the dishes are made in Switzerland. But Emmenthal or Gruyère, which are generally available can be used for most recipes.

The Swiss can serve a varied board from Swiss cheeses exclusively, offering a wide choice. Just a few are Appenzell, and Appenzeller Raess, an aromatic autumn speciality, particularly recommended to be eaten in company with cider and unfermented young wine; Vacherin, also an autumn and winter speciality—a robust cousin of French Camembert—and Fribourg Vacherin; Piora and Valle Maggia, two cheeses from the Tessin; Bündner goat's milk cheese; Urner mountain cheese; Jura cheese; Gomser or Val de Bagne; Wallis cheese, which is also used in the production of Raclette, and Wallis grating cheese; Sbrinz, a hard cheese, like Parmesan, and used not only for grating but also on the cheese board; Bellelay; Schabzieger, a herb cheese—and many others.

CHEESE SOUPS

The dish which in Switzerland was known as 'Cheese Soup' was really a thick mixture of bread and cheese, in which the spoon stood upright. Served with onions fried in butter, it probably contained more calories than a complete dinner of several courses. The following recipes are slightly modified to suit modern tastes.

Urner Cheese Soup *Urner Käsesuppe*

1½ oz. butter or fat
2½ oz. flour
1¾ pints water
1 tablespoon caraway seeds
salt
pepper
nutmeg
garlic to taste
good ½ pint milk
4 oz. grated Emmenthal cheese

Fry flour in butter or fat till golden-brown, add water, spices and seasonings, allow to cook on a low heat for 40–60 minutes. Pour grated cheese into soup tureen and stir in hot milk. Pour soup over cheese mixture and serve.

Bündner Cheese Soup *Bündner Käsesuppe*

4 oz. grated Emmenthal cheese
5 tablespoons milk or cream
2 eggs
2–3 stale rolls, crumbled
salt
2½ pints beef stock
parsley

Blend grated cheese with the cream or milk and pour into soup dish. Mix beaten eggs with the crumbled rolls, salt, and add to boiling stock. Bring to boil and immediately remove saucepan from heat. Now add the boiling soup to cheese, etc. in dish and sprinkle with chopped parsley.

FONDUES

Fondue should really head the procession of cheese dishes by reason of its fame. From being a speciality of the cantons of western Switzerland it has, over the years, become a truly national dish. There are several variants, the best known of which is Fondue Neuchâtel. (Recipes for Fondue Bourguignonne and Fondue Chinoise, which extend the 'dip' method to meat cookery, appear on pages 37–39.)

Fondue Neuchâtel *Fondue Neuchâtel*

Per person:

2½ fl. oz. sparkling white wine
clove of garlic
5½ oz. grated or fine-shredded cheese (half Emmenthal, half Gruyère)
1 level teaspoon cornflour
1 small wine glass Kirsch
shake of pepper
nutmeg or paprika
approx. 6 oz. white bread

In Switzerland, fondue is usually prepared in what is called a 'caquelon', an earthenware dish with a handle, glazed inside; but any enamelled saucepan with a handle may be used, or a not-too-shallow fireproof dish. Rub inside of the saucepan or dish with ½ clove garlic, and warm the wine. Pour cheese into dish and slowly stir in wine until the cheese melts. Now stir Kirsch into the cornflour, add to the cheese and keep stirring over heat until the mixture comes to the boil. Add freshly ground pepper, and nutmeg or paprika according to taste.

You may already know the right way to eat fondue, but if not, here is a description. There should be no more than five at the table. Each guest has a plate and a long fondue fork. In the middle of the table, easily reached from each place, is the spirit heater with the fondue simmering on top. The heater must be regulated so that the fondue is kept gently simmering, never cooling down and never boiling. The bread, which has been cut in cubes shortly before the meal, is arranged in a small basket. Each guest takes a number of pieces of bread, impales one at a time on his fork and dips it into the hot fondue, guiding the fork skilfully back to his mouth without dripping, or decorating the table with threads of cheese. If you lose your bread in the fondue, tradition demands that you stand a round of wine. Fondue is usually served with white wine, but some connoisseurs assert that it is more easily digested if taken with unsweetened tea instead of wine, and a glass of Kirsch to round off.

Fondue Waadtland *Fondue Waadtland*

Ingredients as for Fondue Neuchâtel, but only Gruyère cheese should really be used, and butter is added.

Sauté the garlic in butter for a few moments before adding the wine. The method of preparation is the same as for Fondue Neuchâtel, but the resulting mixture may be a little more liquid.

Fondue Geneva *Fondue Geneva*

This is a creamy cheese mixture that can be served with toast but is also delicious with pasta, or potatoes boiled in their jackets.

1 lb. 2 oz. grated Emmenthal or Gruyère cheese
2½ fl. oz. cream
3–4 egg yolks
½ wine glass white wine
pepper
nutmeg

Mix grated cheese and other ingredients in fireproof fondue dish. Stir over lowest possible heat until the mixture melts and begins to thicken. It must *not* be allowed to boil, or it will curdle. Serve in fireproof dish, keep warm.

Fonduta *Fonduta*

[Tessin]

Like Fondue Geneva, Fonduta is a thick, creamy cheese sauce; in the mountain valleys of the Tessin it is still occasionally served on fast days as an addition to Polenta.

2 oz. butter
2 oz. grated Sbrinz or other cheese
2 oz. Gruyère cheese, fine-sliced or shredded
3 eggs
10 fl. oz. milk
salt
pepper
nutmeg

Mix all ingredients in fireproof dish. Heat mixture slowly, while stirring all the time with a wooden spoon. Be careful not to let it boil. When hot, pour over Polenta (p. 64) and serve at once.

Fried Cheese *Raclette*

[Canton Wallis]

Johanna Spyri described the prototype of all Swiss national dishes made from melted cheese in *Heidi*, in a famous scene when the old grandfather fries the cheese at an open fire. Basically, Raclette is just that—cheese fried in the fire; and in Wallis, and many restaurants all over Switzerland, this speciality is prepared at an open wood fire. A mature Gomser cheese is halved and the cut side held in the flames till the surface begins to melt. The melting cheese is scraped on to a warm plate—*racler* means to scrape—and eaten with small potatoes, salt cucumbers and onions pickled in vinegar. Raclette can easily be made at an open fire in the sitting-room. Preferably use Tilsit or Gruyère: a fairly big piece. Fix on the end of a toasting fork, hold in the flames, and scrape off the melted cheese. In Switzerland there are electric Raclette stoves to put on the dining table, not as romantic as an open fire, but not as hot and messy, either.

To make an easy and equally tasty, if not quite so genuine Raclette, butter the inside of a fireproof dish, remove rind from slices of Tilsit or other cheese and place in dish. Brush very thinly with egg yolk, and allow cheese to melt in a very hot oven. Cheese slices prepared as above can be cooked in a grill-pan or silicated frying pan.

Cheese Steak *Beefsteak au fromage*

[Geneva]

This Cheese Steak could perhaps more properly be classed as a cheese fritter, but is quite unlike the bread-and-cheese fritters described further on. In any case *Beefsteak au fromage* is the name given to it in many Geneva restaurants, though with a true steak it has only its name in common. Though it is quite simple, the preparation needs a little practice.

4–6 oblong slices Gruyère cheese, just under ½-inch thick (if possible, without holes)
good ¼ pint beer
good ¼ pint water
8 oz. plain flour
2 egg whites
oil

Mix beer and water and slowly blend with the flour to make a fairly thick batter. Leave at kitchen temperature for 2 hours. Fold 2 lightly beaten egg whites into the batter. Dust cheese slices lightly with flour so that batter will stick. Heat oil, which must be very hot for batter to form a crust round the cheese immediately. Dip cheese slices into batter and then, one at a time, in the oil. Fry till golden-brown. Lift out carefully and drain on a cloth or absorbent paper. Serve at once on hot plates. The cheese should ooze slowly from the golden-brown crust.

BREAD-AND-CHEESE PUDDING

Ramequin is a generic name for a sort of pudding made from bread and cheese of which there are a number of varieties. They offer a delicious method of using up cheese and bread left over.

Here are two recipes, one using grated, the other sliced cheese.

Bread Pudding with Grated Cheese

Ramequin mit geriebenem Käse

4 eggs
15 fl. oz. cream (or half cream, half milk)
5 oz. grated Gruyère cheese
salt
5 slices white bread
2½ oz. butter

Fry bread in butter until pale golden and place in buttered pie dish. Stir egg yolks into the cream (or cream and milk), add grated cheese and little salt, fold in beaten egg whites and pour some of the mixture on each slice of bread. Bake in hot oven until golden (425°F./Gas mark 7) and serve at once.

Bread Pudding with Sliced Cheese

Ramequin mit Käsescheiben

8 slices bread
8 slices Gruyère cheese
2 eggs
1 pint milk
salt
nutmeg

Place alternate layers of bread and cheese, with the slices overlapping in each layer, in a buttered pie dish. Finish with a layer of cheese. Mix together milk, eggs, salt and nutmeg, and pour over the bread and cheese. Stand pie dish in a *bain-marie* and bake for 30 minutes in a hot oven (425°F./Gas mark 7).

Cheese Balls *Chäs-Happech*

[Appenzell]

Two kinds of cheese are native to Appenzell, one similar to Tilsit and one with a sharp tang which goes very well with young wine. For the following recipe a sharp, well-flavoured cheese should be used. It may be as successfully prepared with Gruyère, but in that case needs a little more seasoning. Try mixing 2 parts Gruyère to 1 part herb cheese if obtainable, to give a very similar result; or experiment with different combinations.

5¾ oz. sharp cheese
good ¼ pint milk
good ¼ pint beer
½ teaspoon baking powder
3–4 oz. plain flour
4 eggs
fat or oil

Shred or dice the cheese. Warm milk, add the cheese and stir over low heat until melted. Allow mixture to cool. Stir flour and baking powder into the beer until smooth and add to the milk. Add the raw eggs one at a time. The resulting batter is a little thicker than ordinary pancake batter. Heat fat or oil in a deep pan and pour in the batter through a funnel to form small spiral-shaped heaps. Fry slowly till golden-brown, drain on paper. These cheese balls may be served with vegetables or a salad, or as a piquant snack with a glass of wine, cider or beer.

CHEESE CAKE

An unsweetened dough, preferably made with yeast, is the foundation. The filling consists of cheese, eggs, milk or cream or—latterly—yoghurt, with the possible addition of chopped onions. Here are two variations.

Basic Cheese Cake *Käsewähe*

1 lb. dough (p. 76)
3 oz. butter
1 oz. plain flour
1¼ pints milk
5 fl. oz. yoghurt
8 oz. grated cheese (half Emmenthal, half Gruyère)
4 eggs
1 chopped cooked onion (optional)
nutmeg

Knead butter into the dough. For the filling, blend flour smoothly with milk and allow to boil for 5 minutes, stirring constantly, before adding the other ingredients. Leave dough for short time in a warm place to rise. Roll out and lay over greased, edged baking sheet. Spread filling on the dough to a thickness of about ¾ inch and bake in a hot oven (425°F./Gas mark 7) for about 40 minutes.

Appenzell Cheese Cake *Appenzeller Käsfladen*

9 oz. plain flour
10 fl. oz. cream or sour cream
2½ fl. oz. milk
1 large grated onion
10 oz. shredded Gruyère cheese
1 egg
1 lb. dough (see p. 76)
3 oz. butter

Follow directions for the Basic Cheese Cake above; but instead of boiling milk and flour, mix all the cold ingredients for the filling together into a thick paste, spread over dough and bake (425°F. Gas mark) for 40 minutes.

Cheese Tarts *Käsepastetchen*

These are best eaten fresh from the oven, but they can also be reheated.

10 oz. puff paste or shortcrust pastry
5½ oz. grated cheese (half Emmenthal, half Gruyère)
1 tablespoon cornflour
good ¼ pint cream or milk
2 eggs
salt
nutmeg

Roll out paste very thinly and line 12 small bun tins. Sprinkle half the grated cheese over pastry in tins. Mix rest of cheese with other ingredients and fill tins two-thirds full. Bake in preheated oven (425°F./Gas mark 7) for 20 minutes.

Semolina Cakes with Cheese Filling [Fribourg] *Griesskückhlein mit Käse gefüllt*

1¾ pints milk
salt
5½ oz. semolina
sliced Gruyère cheese
1 egg
1 oz. flour
1 tablespoon breadcrumbs
fat

Bring milk to the boil, add salt, stir in semolina and cook for 15–20 minutes to a thick paste, stirring well meanwhile. Spread the hot paste on a china plate first rinsed in cold water, or on a dampened wooden board, and allow to cool. When cold, stamp out round shapes with an upturned glass, lid, or cutter; and use the same to cut cheese rounds from the slices. Place 1 cheese round between 2 slices of paste. Dip the 'sandwiches' first in beaten egg, then in breadcrumbs mixed with flour, and fry in hot fat till golden-brown on both sides.

CHEESE FRITTERS

Of all the Swiss cheese specialities, these bread-and-cheese recipes are perhaps the most certain to be incorporated into your everyday menus. They are easy to make, and the variations are infinite. No elaborate preparations are needed and there is no difficulty in cooking small portions. Try one of these delicious fritters as a savoury to round off the meal, as well.

Waadtland Cheese Fritters *Käseschnitten Waadtländer Art*

4 slices 1⅜-inch-thick toast
2½ fl. oz. white wine
5½ oz. grated Gruyère cheese
1 egg
paprika
pepper

Moisten the slices of toast with a little of the wine and arrange on a baking sheet. Mix rest of the wine with the cheese, egg and spices to a fairly thick paste and spread on the toast. Sprinkle with more paprika and pepper. Bake briefly in a very hot oven (445°F./Gas mark 8) until cheese begins to melt; serve at once.

Basle Cheese Fritters *Käseschnitten Basler Art*

4 slices bread
1 oz. butter
3 onions
4 slices Gruyère or Emmenthal cheese
paprika

Fry bread lightly on both sides in butter and arrange on a baking sheet. Pour boiling water over finely chopped onions and leave for a moment. Pour off water, and fry onions in remains of the butter until tender. Spread onions thinly on the bread and cover each slice with a slice of cheese. Sprinkle with paprika and bake in a very hot oven (445°F./Gas mark 8) until cheese melts; serve at once.

Bern Cheese Fritters *Käseschnitten Berner Art*

8 oz. grated Gruyère cheese
2 eggs
2½ fl. oz. milk
1 teaspoon Kirsch
fat for frying
6–8 slices bread

Mix grated cheese with the egg yolks, milk and Kirsch. Fold in beaten egg whites, and spread mixture on bread. Heat fat in a large frying pan and place bread, cheese side down, in hot fat. When the slices swell and become golden-brown, turn and fry briefly on the other side.

Emmenthal Cheese Fritters *Käseschnitten Emmentaler Art*

Per person:

1 large slice bread
1 slice ham
1 tablespoon butter
1 slice Emmenthal cheese
salt
pepper
1 egg

Lightly toast the bread. Fry the ham briefly, place on bread, cover with cheese and season. Place in a fairly hot oven to allow cheese to melt, or in covered frying pan on top of the cooker. At the last moment, top cheese with a fried egg.

St Gallen Cheese Fritters *Käseschnitten St Galler Art*

4 oz. pork sausage meat
4 thin slices bread
8 thin slices Tilsit or Gruyère cheese
pepper
1 egg
breadcrumbs or flour
fat for frying

Spread sausage meat on both sides of each slice of bread. Place each slice between two cheese slices, top and bottom, and press all well together. Sprinkle with pepper, brush with beaten egg and coat with breadcrumbs. Leave for a few minutes for the coating to dry, then fry slices in deep fat on both sides.

Other Ideas for Fritters

1. Add fried tomatoes or steamed mushrooms.
2. Mix cheese with tiny pieces of bacon.
3. Give fritters an oriental flavour by adding half a banana fried in butter and sprinkling with curry powder.
4. Spread left-over spinach on toast and cover with a slice of cheese.

Cheese Kebabs with Processed Gruyère Cheese

Käsespiesschen mit Schachtelkäse

This, of course, is not an old recipe since the processing and packaging of cheese is an invention of our time. But, as tried and approved by Swiss experts, it can be thoroughly recommended.

Per person:

1 portion processed Gruyère cheese	flour
2–3 slices white bread	1 egg yolk
milk	oil

Cut 4 triangular slices from the one cheese portion. Cut bread into triangles of roughly the same size. On a wooden meat skewer arrange alternate slices of bread and cheese, finishing with bread. Dip skewer first in milk, then in flour and lastly in beaten egg. Fry in smoking-hot oil. The Cheese Kebabs should be not too crisp, and still a little soft. Serve with a salad, or tomato sauce.

'Cheese Quarrels' *Käsegezanke*

[Graubünden]

Another of the many bread-and-cheese-recipes, for which many different kinds of cheese may be used.

9 oz. thin-sliced rye bread
6 oz. Emmenthal or other cheese
10 fl. oz. slightly salted water
2 oz. butter

Cut both bread and cheese in narrow strips, fill dish with alternate layers of bread and cheese, and pour over water. Cover dish and leave to stand for 15 minutes till water is mostly absorbed. Pour off surplus water. Fry the bread-and-cheese-mixture in fat till golden-brown; or simply pour over sizzling, brown melted butter, and serve.

Cheese Salad *Käsesalat*

This makes a splendid snack after theatre or cinema, or at any other time; and there are countless variations that will produce a main dish or hors d'oeuvre or whatever you wish. Add grapes, bananas, nuts, pears, asparagus, hard-boiled eggs, olives, salami, and so on; but try this simple recipe first.

9 oz. Emmenthal cut in paper-thin slices

Dressing:

4 tablespoons oil
2 tablespoons vinegar
1 finely chopped onion
1 teaspoon mustard
1 teaspoon caraway seeds
salt
pepper
paprika

Mix all ingredients for the dressing, which may be more or less sharp according to taste. Put cheese into the dressing to soak for at least 1 hour. Serve with beer or cider.

Eastern Switzerland is the real home of Cheese Salads, especially the canton of Thurgau. You may even be introduced, in some farmhouse, to the custom known as 'Stupfete'. A salad dressing similar to the one above, but without caraway seeds, is placed in the middle of the table. Each participant has a large piece of cheese in front of him on the scrubbed wooden table. He cuts off pieces of the cheese—occasionally alternating with potatoes cooked in the jacket—spears them with his fork and dips them in the common bowl of dressing. Try it and see!

FISH FOR THE GOURMET

Inn at Lake Zug

Though fish has never been a staple food in Switzerland, the fish from Swiss lakes, rivers and streams have always been highly prized by the gourmet and prepared in particularly delicious ways. The best of these recipes, including some which originated in other countries but which the Swiss have made their own, are given here.

First a word about the most common kinds of fish, though in the recipes that follow, any available freshwater fish can be substituted (or in the last resort, white sea fish).

The *Felchen* or whitefish, which the French call *féra*, are found in all Swiss lakes. The blue variety from Lake Constance and Lake Neuchâtel are even tastier than the silver kinds—the small 'Bondelles', and larger 'Ballen' or 'Balchen'. All have firm, white flesh and are delicacies which, if only they were rarer and therefore more expensive, would be highly regarded as such.

The next most important fish, the *Egli* (the French *perche*), is a freshwater perch found in rivers and greatly esteemed by connoisseurs.

Forellen are trout, and blue trout appears on the menu of all good restaurants; but unfortunately the fish are mostly bred in captivity and their flavour does not compare with that of their ancestors, the river trout. In the valleys of Tessin 'real' trout are still to be had, among the rocks of mountain streams, though the hydro-electric plants which dam the water of these streams are having ill effects. However, to comfort connoisseurs there yet remain the large lake trout and the Rhine trout.

The *Aeschi* is only caught in late autumn and winter, either in the Rhine or in certain other rivers. It is a cousin of the trout and just as tasty.

A distant relative of the trout is the delicious *Rötel* with its red underside, also caught in late autumn and winter. It should be eaten when freshly caught. Some prefer the Rötel of Lake Zug to that of Lake Lugano, while in Geneva they swear by the '*Omble Chevalier*' (caught in Lake Thun as well).

Tench, eel and carp (*Schleien*, *Aale* and *Karpfen*) are caught in Switzerland but are not particularly popular, though the *Trüsche* or eel pout is much in favour: the liver, fried in butter and served with lemon juice, is considered a delicacy. The pike (*Hecht*) is highly valued—though its many bones frighten the lazy or timid. Fried and served with a mayonnaise sauce it takes pride of place in many fish restaurants.

If you like fish, you cannot do better than tour the lakes of western Switzerland—Lake Biel or Lake Geneva, for instance—during the wine harvest. In the little inns along the lake shores you will get freshly pressed grape juice, known as 'Sauser', with fish fried or cooked according to local custom—fish that is fresher than fresh . . . .

Fried Salmon *Lachs nach Basler Art*
[Basle]

one 2½–3 lb. salmon
salt
pepper
flour
2 oz. butter
2 onions
2½ fl. oz. white wine or beef stock
lemon
parsley

Clean and wash fish in the usual way, and dry. Cut in strips about the thickness of a thumb, sprinkle with salt, pepper and flour. Fry quickly till golden in 1 oz. butter, turning the pieces gently in the pan to avoid breaking. Place carefully on a warm plate and keep warm in the oven. Cut onions in slices and fry till tender in 1 oz. butter. Pour over the fish. Boil the white wine or little beef stock in the same pan; pour over the fish. Garnish with lemon and parsley, and serve.

Rötel with Wine Sauce *R¨tel nach Zuger Art*
[Zug]

Per person:

2 small fish
15 fl. oz. white wine
1 oz. butter
1 dessertspoon flour
herbs (parsley, rosemary, thyme, sage, marjoram)
1 small onion or shallot
salt

Bring white wine to the boil in a saucepan, add the cleaned and prepared fish; bring to the boil once more, then remove from heat and leave saucepan, covered, to stand for 5 minutes. Melt butter in small pan, add finely chopped onion, flour and finely chopped herbs, and allow to cook for a few minutes. Pour in wine from the fish pan and stir all until smooth. Add salt to taste. Let the fish simmer for another 5–10 minutes in this sauce, and serve with boiled potatoes.

Larded Pike *Gespickter Hecht nach Basler Art*

[Basle]

Whereas carp and tench are not very popular in Switzerland, pike is eaten with great relish. It is usually cut into slices, dipped in milk and flour and fried in deep fat, then served with mayonnaise. The following recipe comes from Basle.

approx. 3-lb. pike
salt
2 oz. bacon strips for larding
2 oz. anchovies
3¾ oz. butter
2 tablespoons lemon juice
2 tablespoons Madeira
good ¼ pint beef stock
1 tablespoon capers

Clean and dry the pike, sprinkle with salt and lard* with bacon and strips of anchovy. Tie together head and tail, so that the fish forms a ring, and place in baking dish, with butter cut in pieces. Sprinkle with lemon juice. Bake in medium-hot oven for 1–1½ hours (355°F./Gas mark 4). Baste also frequently with butter, from time to time adding a little Madeira and stock. If the pike gets too brown, cover with buttered greaseproof paper. When cooked, place pike on a warm plate to keep hot. If necessary, dilute the sauce with stock. Bring to the boil; then pass through a sieve, add capers and fine strips of anchovy, and turn into sauceboat to serve with the fish.

Baked Whitefish *Zuger Ballen*

[Zug]

Any large fish may be prepared in the same manner.

1 large fish
salt
pepper
sage leaves
3¾ oz. butter
1 onion
cloves
¾ oz. flour
1 wine glass white wine
parsley

Clean fish, dry, and sprinkle inside and out with salt and pepper.

* Larding consists of threading lardoons of varying thickness into meat, fish, etc. with a larding needle.

Make a few cuts on the back and insert the sage leaves. Melt two-thirds of the butter in an oblong casserole or baking dish, put in the fish, with the onion stuck with cloves. Sprinkle fish with flour, add rest of the butter in pieces and bake in preheated oven (400°F./Gas mark 6). Baste from time to time with melted butter. After 20 minutes, add the wine and a small bunch of parsley. Cook for a further 15 minutes.

Perch or Whitefish *à la meunière* (without almonds)

Egli oder Felchen à la meunière ohne Mandeln

The method of cooking '*à la meunière*' is, of course, no Swiss speciality, any more than the recipe with almonds given below; but both are so popular as to have acquired Swiss nationality.

- whole or filleted fish (enough for 4)
- 4 dessertspoons milk
- 1 oz. flour
- 2 oz. butter or oil
- lemon juice
- 2 oz. unsalted butter
- chopped parsley
- lemon slices

Clean and dry the fish. Dip first in milk, then coat with flour and salt mixed. The flour covering should be quite thin and milk is therefore preferable to the usual egg as a base. Before frying the fish, put serving dish to warm, have lemon juice squeezed ready and the parsley chopped, because everything has to be done very quickly once fish is ready. Fry fish on both sides in butter or oil till golden-brown, arrange on warm dish and sprinkle with lemon juice. Put 2 oz. fresh butter in frying pan. Scrape up the bits in the pan, then fry the parsley in the butter for 10 seconds and pour mixture over the fish. Garnish with slices of lemon.

Perch or Whitefish with Almonds

Egli oder Felchen mit Mandeln

This dish is served in western Switzerland under the name of *Filet de Perche aux amandes*. Preparation is exactly as in the recipe above, but the parsley is replaced by thin slices of almond fried till light brown in butter or oil.

Fish with Brown Sauce *Fische nach Walchwiler Art*
[Canton Zug]

Walchwil is situated on the banks of Lake Zug, between Zug and Arth Goldau. It is a pretty village whose fish restaurants are renowned all over Switzerland. The fish of Lake Zug are served either with a sauce made with white wine and herbs, or *nach Walchwiler Art*—in a brown sauce. These recipes are, of course, family secrets, which can only be given approximately; each housewife adds her own special touches: small amounts of herbs, or tiny quantities of spices, which make the dish her own.

fish for 4 (filleted)
1 oz. flour
1¼ oz. butter
1 wine glass red wine
15 fl. oz. water
2 onions
2 cloves
2 bay leaves
lemon rind
salt, pepper

Fry flour in butter till light brown, stirring well to avoid lumps. Pour in water and wine. Stick a clove in each onion, add with bay leaves and lemon rind, season. Allow sauce to simmer for 1 hour on lowest possible heat. Cook the prepared fish in the sauce for 15 minutes, then serve immediately.

Whitefish with Herb Sauce
Felchen im eigenen Saft mit Kräutersauce

Any really fresh fish can be used for this dish. You need a double saucepan for steaming.

2 medium-sized fish
salt
pepper
lemon juice
1 pint Béchamel sauce
2 dessertspoons cream
chopped herbs (parsley, dill, basil, chives)

Pour 1½ inches water into the bottom half of a fairly large steamer. When top half is on, the water should not reach the bottom of the grid, even when boiling. Half an hour before cooking, rub fish inside and out with salt, pepper and lemon juice. Steam until tender, topping up with water in the meantime if necessary.

(When the back fin can be pulled away easily and cleanly, the fish is done.) Add what remains of the water in the steamer to the Béchamel sauce—the water will have absorbed some of the juice and flavour of the fish. Stir in the cream. Add plenty of chopped fresh herbs to the sauce and pour part over the fish, serving the rest separately.

Trout in Geneva Sauce *Forellen mit Genfer Sauce*

For this dish the Genevans use the Rötel from Lake Geneva, but it is just as good with trout, particularly the larger lake trout.

1 large or several small trout
1 oz. butter
3 shallots
salt
pepper
white wine (according to size of pan)
lemon juice

For the sauce:

2 oz. butter
2 oz. flour
salt, pepper
1–2 egg yolks
1 tablespoon milk

Sauté the shallots lightly in butter. Clean and prepare the fish, sprinkle with salt and pepper, add to shallots and pour in white wine (or half wine, half water) till the fish are about half covered. Sprinkle with lemon juice, and allow to simmer very slowly until tender. Lift fish out carefully and keep warm on a preheated dish. Melt 1¼ oz. butter in a small pan, add flour and cook till light brown. Sieve and stir in the wine in which fish have cooked and allow to boil until thickened. Blend egg yolks and milk together and blend into the sauce. Add rest of the butter, and whisk till the sauce is almost boiling. Pour over the fish to serve.

Mixed Fried Fish *Friture du lac*

Fresh-caught small fish, fried in deep fat, are a speciality along the shores of Lake Biel and Lake Neuchâtel. Most often the fish are just salted, dipped in milk, rolled in flour and then fried in oil. Or they can be fried in batter as follows.

good ¼ pint light ale
5½ oz. plain flour
2 egg whites
1 tablespoon oil
1 level teaspoon salt
lemon slices

Mix all ingredients except egg whites and lemon and leave for 1–2 hours. Immediately before use, fold in stiffly beaten egg whites. Dip fish in batter, fry, drain well, then serve immediately. Garnish with plenty of lemon.

Pike in Tomato Sauce

[Tessin] *Hecht in Tomatensauce nach Tessiner Art*

This recipe is particularly suitable for a large fish, especially if it is inclined to be tough.

1 large pike
2 pints tomato sauce
salt
herbs (marjoram, basil, thyme, sage, rosemary)

Make a fairly thin tomato sauce, and add herbs. Season. Simmer whole pike slowly in this sauce for 1–1½ hours, according to size of fish.

Pickled Fish *Agoni in Carpione*

[Tessin]

This is usually made with the 'Agoni' caught in Lake Lugano, which are about 6–8 inches long. In the inns along the lake shore, these are usually served *in carpione* and taste something like pickled herrings, though the addition of many different herbs and spices makes the flavour more piquant.

2–4 lb. fish
salt
flour
cooking oil
herbs (rosemary, sage, marjoram, thyme, parsley)
2 onions
1 carrot
4 cloves
3 bay leaves
1 pint white vinegar
10 fl. oz. red wine

Rub the cleaned and prepared fish with salt, dust with flour and fry in a shallow pan of oil, together with a little rosemary and 2 sage leaves, until golden-yellow. Place in shallow dish or casserole. For the marinade, slice onions in rings and fry in 2 dessertspoons of the oil in which fish were fried, with the chopped herbs (not too much of each), shredded carrot, cloves and bay leaves (if no fresh herbs are available, use dried ones, but do not fry these). Pour in the wine and vinegar, bring to the boil and pour over the fish, which should be completely covered. Keep in a cool place for 2–3 days, and serve the fish as an entrée.

MEAT AND POULTRY DISHES

Fondue Bourguignonne

The Swiss of today are considerable meat-eaters—and discerning ones who know what's good when they see it. Yet there are only a few typically Swiss meat dishes, for in past centuries meat was not a staple food, but reserved for Sundays and feast days and important family occasions. In districts where pigs were bred, their slaughter was the occasion for a feast when, for once, there was as much fresh meat as you could want. Otherwise meat was usually smoked or pickled. On the other hand, as in most country cooking, the stews offer a real goldmine for gourmets.

Stockpot *Pot-au-feu*

Petite marmite—Pot-au-feu—Siedfleisch—Bollito misto: the stockpot has many names. *Pot-au-feu* is a speciality on the menu of many Swiss restaurants, who usually combine the beef with a boiling chicken, a juicy marrow bone and extras like grated horseradish, bilberries, small slices of toast, gherkins, beetroot and boiled potatoes. In the average household, *Pot-au-feu* can be served in two ways: as a stew with meat, vegetables and marrow bone served together in the gravy, or as two separate courses, first the beef broth, preferably accompanied by toast, and then the beef itself surrounded by whole vegetables, a feast for the eye as well as the stomach.

3–4 scraped carrots
1 head celery, sliced
1 savoy cabbage
2 leeks cut in 3-inch pieces
1 onion stuck with 4 cloves
2 tomatoes (optional)
½ fennel root (optional)
meat extract or stock cubes (optional)
few soup bones (optional)
small piece of liver
piece of oxtail
4–5 pints water
salt
2½–3 lb. stewing meat, with some, but not too much fat
2 marrow bones
little saffron or soy sauce (optional)

Put all vegetables, except the tomatoes, with the liver, oxtail and soup bones, in saucepan of cold water. Add salt. If possible, avoid using an aluminium saucepan. It is advisable to place the bones in a small bag so that no splinters get into the broth. Bring water to the boil, then add the meat. Bring to the boil once more, but from then on the soup should just simmer. According to the amount of meat, simmer for between 2–3 hours. If vegetables are tender earlier, lift them out carefully and put aside to be added again shortly before serving. After half the cooking time add the marrow bones, and towards the end the tomatoes. Should the soup not be strong enough—it depends very much on the quality of the meat—add meat extract or beef stock made from cubes. Saffron gives an attractive yellow colour, or a few drops of soy sauce a brown colouring to the soup.

Bernese Board *Berner Platte*

The authoress of an American cookery book visited Switzerland and expressed her desire to be introduced to some typically Swiss dishes. On three successive days, she was invited to a meal in three different places. Three times she was offered the *Berner Platte*, or 'Bernese Board', and she probably thinks that the Swiss live exclusively on sauerkraut and smoked pork!

The dish is deservedly popular, can be easily adapted and will not unduly tax anyone's cooking skill. The basis of sauerkraut is prepared in the usual way, with or without juniper berries, and with or without the addition of white wine.

The dish owes its fame to its overwhelming copiousness. It is a proud demonstration of abundance, a relic from the days when good times were followed by lean times, when people were generous and liked to show that they could afford to be so. The Bernese Board in its full glory can still be ordered at any of the beautiful old inns of the Emmenthal. On a large platter piled high, a small amount of sauerkraut is just visible in the centre. The rest is covered with ribs of pork, boiled bacon, boiled beef or other meat and thick slices of Bernese tongue sausage, with perhaps a few small pork sausages, smoked tongue and ham. There will be boiled potatoes and in some places, a dish of French beans, which in summertime may replace the sauerkraut altogether. Other meats combine equally well with the sauerkraut.

Braised Cabbage with Mutton *Urner Häfelikabis*

The Swiss name needs some explanation: a 'häfeli' is a small saucepan, and *kabis* means cabbage.

1 lb. 2 oz. stewing mutton
1 lb. 2 oz. stewing pork
1¼ oz. butter or fat
2–3 onions
1 large cabbage
1 pint beef stock
salt
pepper
1¾ lb. potatoes

Cut meat in pieces and fry in hot fat; put on one side. Lightly fry the chopped onions in the same fat till tender. Shred cabbage and add to the onions. Keep turning the cabbage in the saucepan until lightly browned, pour in the stock, add the meat, season and leave to simmer in saucepan with well-fitting lid for at least 15 minutes. Then add the raw potatoes, peeled and halved, top up with liquid if necessary and leave to cook until the potatoes are done (do not allow them to break).

Braised Leg of Mutton *Schafstotzen im Becki*

[Graubünden]

The name indicates a leg of mutton baked in the oven with potatoes and vegetables. The 'becki' is the pan in which it is cooked, preferably of copper. It will serve about 8.

1 well-hung leg of mutton
salt
pepper
clove of garlic
2 oz. fat
8 oz. carrots
1 onion stuck with 2 cloves
1 chopped onion
approx. ½ pint water or stock
2¼ lb. potatoes

If you have no really large frying pan, ask the butcher to fillet the leg of mutton. Beat the meat thoroughly, rub with salt and pepper, put a few small pieces of garlic in the meat and, if filleted, tie it into a roll. Fry quickly all over in hot fat, add to scraped carrots, the onions and 1 cup water or stock. Cook for 2 hours in the oven (335°F./Gas mark 3) turning and basting frequently. Then add potatoes, cut in half, and leave to cook for another 40–50 minutes. If necessary, add more liquid during the cooking.

Bacon with Dried Apples and Potatoes

[Canton Aargau] *Schnitz und Kartoffeln*

A winter stew, in which dried apples take the place of fresh vegetables. (See also p. 55)

10 oz. dried apples
1–2 tablespoons sugar
approx. 10 oz. bacon or smoked meat (in one piece)
1 lb. 2 oz. potatoes
salt
little butter (optional)

Soak apples in cold water for a few hours, then pour off the water. Let the sugar brown lightly in a dry saucepan, add the drained apples and bacon, cover with cold water and cook gently for 50 minutes. Then add potatoes cut in quarters, salt to taste and continue cooking until potatoes are soft (about 30 minutes). Shake saucepan to mix all ingredients well together. If lean smoked meat is used, a little butter can be added.

In the canton of Lucerne, a similar dish is made with fresh pears. First parboil the bacon. Lightly brown the sugar with a little butter, pour in the water in which bacon was cooked, add quartered pears and finally the potatoes and cook till both are tender.

Bacon Stew with Young Peas *Chifelstunggis*

'*Chifel*' is a Swiss name for young peas in the pod.

2 onions
clove of garlic (optional)
2 teaspoons cooking fat
2¼ lb. young peas in the pod
3¾ oz. diced bacon
salt
1½ lb. potatoes
chopped parsley

Fry the chopped onions and crushed garlic in fat until tender; add the washed and drained pods and bacon and a little water, salt, and allow to cook slowly. Shake saucepan from time to time to prevent pods from sticking. After 20 minutes, add the diced potatoes and, if necessary, more water and continue cooking gently till potatoes are done. Sprinkle with chopped parsley, and serve.

Swiss Bean and Mutton Stew *Innerschweiz Bohnentopf*

14 oz. stewing mutton
1 oz. fat
10 oz. carrots, cut in strips
approx. 1 pint water

piece of bacon
2¼ lb. haricot or broad beans
2¼ lb. potatoes
salt

Fry mutton quickly in hot fat, add the bacon cut up roughly, beans, carrots and about 1 pint water. Simmer slowly in covered saucepan for 30 minutes. Add peeled potatoes cut in half. Taste and, if necessary, add salt (it depends on the bacon) and continue cooking until potatoes are soft.

Pork Stew *Stunggis*
[Canton Unterwalden]

1 lb. 2 oz. diced pork
2 leeks
1 large onion
1 small cabbage
2–3 carrots
salt
1 lb. 2 oz. potatoes, cut in pieces

Fill saucepan with alternate layers of meat and of vegetables cut fine; add water and salt. Cover closely and cook for 30 minutes. Add potatoes; if necessary, top up with water and cook until done.

Leak and Sausage Stew (see p. 50)

Fondue Bourguignonne *Fondue Bourguignonne*

Since the Second World War a new Swiss dish has become a national favourite. Fondue Bourguignonne is ideally suited to modern informal entertaining. It needs no great preparation and is cooked, served and eaten at the table. People started inviting each other to a Fondue Bourguignonne; famous restaurants added 'Chef's Special—Fondue Bourguignonne' to the menu; stores sold special equipment for Fondue Bourguignonne and handkerchiefs and cloths were printed with the recipe.

Strictly, this is no 'fondue', for nothing melts; nor is the name 'Bourguignonne' deserved since it neither comes from Burgundy nor uses red wine—for which the cookery term is '*à la bourguignonne*'. But it does use small pieces of beef as in the French *Bœuf à la Bourguignonne* and, as in all fondue dishes, the dipping in sauce is the great feature.

- 6–8 oz. fillet of beef, rump steak or roast beef, per person
- $1\frac{1}{8}$–$1\frac{3}{4}$ pints oil or butter or fat
- other ingredients according to taste

Cut meat in 1-inch cubes. Place spirit cooker in centre of the table and on it a small, not-too-shallow cooking dish containing hot oil. This dish should not be pottery or glass, which are too fragile, but either metal or enamelware. It would be dangerous if the dish were to break and spill boiling oil over the table.

Each guest has on his plate a number of raw meat cubes, a wooden skewer, or fondue fork, and an ordinary fork. He spears a meat cube with his skewer, dips it in the hot oil and holds it there for a short time if he likes meat underdone, or longer if he prefers it well done. Since the skewer or fondue fork gets very hot while held in the oil, the cooked meat is then transferred to the other fork.

In Fondue Bourguignonne, however, quite as important as the meat are the sauces and 'extras' with which it is seasoned according to taste. Restaurants usually serve Béarnaise or Tartar sauce and one other savoury sauce, as well as mustard, mixed pickles, tomato ketchup and Worcester sauce. At home, sauces tend to be less complicated and are sometimes replaced by cream cheese blended with herbs or savoury herb butter, mayonnaise, pepper, paprika, gherkins, capers and different spices. The raw meat may be arranged on lettuce leaves, as a contrast. Serve with a large dish of green salad, radishes and celery, and different kinds of bread and biscuits. Other kinds of meat such as fillet of pork, veal, or chipolatas, also lend themselves to the fondue treatment; or mushrooms, sliced peppers and sliced aubergines may be used.

Fondue Chinoise *Fondue Chinoise*

The method is the same as for Fondue Bourguignonne, but instead of hot oil, boiling chicken soup is used. The stock may be made from cubes if desired. This recipe is more easily digestible for those who cannot tolerate fat. The meat—again fillet or rump steak—is cut in strips approx. $1\frac{1}{4} \times 2\frac{1}{2}$ inches. These strips are wrapped round the fork and dipped in the boiling stock. As the meal progresses, the soup increases in flavour and strength, and is served after the meat in small cups. Accompaniments to Fondue Chinoise are the same as for Fondue Bourguignonne.

Roast Fillet of Beef *Lummelbraten*
[Basle]

In the old city of Basle on festive occasions they used to serve a larded joint which compares honourably even with English roast beef or the French Châteaubriand. This serves 10.

2¼ lb. fillet of beef
2 oz. fat pork for larding, cut in strips approx. ⅛ × 1⅛ in.
salt
pepper
2 oz. butter
1 carrot
1 onion
stick of celery
2½ fl. oz. white wine
2½ fl. oz. stock

Unless you are very skilful, ask your butcher to lard, roll and tie the meat. Rub with salt and pepper and fry in hot butter (or half butter, half oil) on all sides until brown. With vegetables, place in tin pan in white wine and stock and place in hot oven (445°F./Gas mark 8). Baste frequently with the gravy.

You should allow 20–30 minutes for roasting, according to thickness of the meat. It should still be pink in the middle. To serve, pour a few spoonfuls of gravy over the meat; then scrape the bits off the bottom of the pan, and, if necessary, add little wine and stock to the gravy to make it enough.

Braised Beef *Stufato alla Chiassese*
[Chiasso]

The beef in this recipe is well seasoned and spicy. It serves 8.

2¼ lb. beef
bacon and garlic for larding
1 oz. flour
1½ oz. butter (or half butter, half oil)
1 onion
1 carrot
rosemary
marjoram
salt
pepper
1 glass white wine
4 tomatoes
1 lb. potatoes

Lard the meat with garlic and bacon, sprinkle with flour and fry all over in hot fat, with the onion, until brown. Season. Add carrot and herbs; pour in white wine, cover and braise for 1½ hours (400°F./Gas mark 6) turning and basting frequently and, if necessary, adding water or stock. Then add peeled potatoes and the tomatoes to the meat, cover again and continue cooking for another 20–30 minutes.

Beef Stew *Rindsvoressen*

In Switzerland, many of the stews have the word *voressen* (or *entrée*) in the name: *Rindsvoressen, Kalbsvoressen* and so on. I discovered why when I was invited to a 'Sichlete' or harvest festival, in the Emmenthal. The meal began with beef broth and then came the stew, in this case mutton, followed by a mixed salad. Only *then* did the 'main dish', a Bernese Board, appear and the 'real meal' began. (It was followed by numerous tarts, fruit and cream!) In normal households, these traditional stews have, naturally, long since become the main dish.

1½ lb. beef (preferably shoulder or neck)
salt
1 oz. fat
2 onions
½ oz. flour
½ glass red wine

Salt meat and fry in fat over strong heat. Lightly brown the chopped onions in a saucepan, add meat, sprinkle with flour and pour in the wine. Cook briskly till the liquid thickens, then add little hot water and cook slowly till meat is ready (approx. 1 hour).

For Pork Stew and Brown Veal Stew, follow the above method, but omit the wine and flour the meat before frying. A little cream makes an excellent addition to the gravy. For a White Veal Stew, cook meat in saucepan of hot salted water without frying, add an onion stuck with cloves. Make a white sauce separately. Add white wine or cream before serving.

Liver on Skewers *Leberspiesschen*
[Zürich]

This dish takes a certain amount of preparation, but the combination of liver, sage and bacon is worth the trouble.

14 oz. calf's liver (or can be ox liver) cut in thin slices
2 oz. very thin-sliced lean bacon
sage
2 oz. butter
1 onion
salt
pepper
thin wood or metal skewers

Skin the liver and cut in slices about ¼ inch thick and 2 inches long. Spike alternate pieces of liver, sage and bacon along the skewers. Chop onion and fry approx. 1 tablespoonful in butter; then add skewers and fry on both sides. This takes no more than 6–8 minutes. Season with salt and pepper and serve with French beans or spinach.

Diced Veal *Geschnetzeltes Kalbfleisch*
[Zürich]

The veal takes only a few minutes to prepare, but should be served immediately it is done, or it will get hard.

1 lb. 2 oz. veal fillets (as for escalopes)
½ oz. flour
1 small onion
2 oz. butter
2½ fl. oz. white wine
salt
pepper
3 tablespoons cream (optional)

Ask your butcher for thin pieces of veal (about thumbnail size), or liver, beef and pork can be equally well prepared in this way. If you have to cut the meat yourself, it must first be freed of any skin, fat and sinew, then cut in thin slices. Cut these in strips and again into smaller pieces (in Switzerland the *geschnetzelte* meat is prepared by the butcher). Sprinkle the veal with flour. Chop onion finely, fry in very hot butter in frying pan till golden-yellow, and add the meat. Fry over strong heat, turning the veal constantly. After about a minute, it should be almost white. Pour in white wine (or half white wine, half stock), season with salt and pepper, leave to cook for 2 minutes and serve. If liked, cream can be added at the last minute. In the old days, pasta and apple sauce were served with the meat. Today it is usually eaten with fried potatoes, though connoisseurs assert that a dry, savoury rice is preferable to anything else.

Diced Liver *Geschnetzelte Leber*

A special favourite with many Swiss: it is usually made from calf's liver, but ox or pig's liver can be used.

14 oz. calf's liver, skinned and cut in small pieces
1 onion
½ oz. flour
1 oz. butter
4 tablespoons white wine
4 tablespoons stock
salt
pepper

Chop onion and fry with the liver in hot butter over strong heat, turning the liver constantly till all the pieces are light brown. Sprinkle with flour, pour in wine and stock, let contents come nearly but *not* quite to the boil, then remove from heat. Add salt, pepper, at this stage, not before, and serve with mashed potatoes, dry rice, scrambled egg.

Stuffed Rabbit *Gefülltes Oster-Gitzi*
[Graubünden]

The following recipe from the Puschlav, one of the Italian-speaking valleys of Graubünden, is traditionally made with young kid, or 'Gitzi' at Easter-time. Rabbit has been substituted, and chicken can equally be used. The recipe serves 8.

2 rabbits
4 bread rolls
4 eggs
2 oz. peeled, chopped almonds
2 oz. raisins
chopped peel of 1 lemon
18 fl. oz. milk
salt, pepper
3¾ oz. butter
onions
rosemary
marjoram
stock or white wine for basting

First prepare the stuffing: finely grate the bread and combine with eggs, almonds, raisins, lemon peel, milk and salt in a fairly fluid mixture. Stuff the rabbits with this and sew up well, or skewer skin together. Pour over hot butter, add onions and herbs, cover and bake in hot oven (400°F./Gas mark 6), basting from time to time with stock or wine, for 2 hours.

Baked Rabbit in Batter *Gitziprägel*
[Graubünden]

14 oz. rabbit or chicken meat, cut in small, flat pieces
1½ oz. butter
thin 3-egg pancake batter (see p. 72)

Plunge meat into boiling water and leave for 3 minutes, then drain. Heat butter in a large pan and fry the meat evenly all over till brown, shaking and turning constantly. Pour over the batter and bake for 1 hour (380°F./Gas mark 5). Serve with salad, or stewed apple, according to taste.

Meat Pasty *Kügelipastete*
[Canton Lucerne]

For 1 large or 2 small pasties:

1 lb. 10 oz. plain flour
10 oz. butter
5 fl. oz. water
salt
2 large and 3 small eggs
1 egg for coating

For the filling:

See recipe for Meat Balls (p. 50)
small pieces of brain (optional)
thin-sliced mushrooms (optional)

For the sauce:

2 oz. butter
2 oz. flour
scant ½ pint white wine
scant ½ pint stock

First rub butter into the flour. Mix with other ingredients for the pasty (except 1 egg for coating) into a dough, and leave for at least 30 minutes in a cool place. Divide dough in two uneven parts, roll out smaller part to approx. ¼-inch thickness, trim circle and lay over a greased baking tin. Brush with egg white around edges of the dough to a depth of approx. ¾ inch. Twist a large white napkin into a spiral; then roll this in a circle and lay it flat on the dough. The napkin serves as the 'false filling' of your pasty and after baking you pull it out by one end, which should be left projecting upwards in the middle of the circle.

Roll out the rest of the dough and lay it over the napkin, so that it lies flat and smooth. Press the edges of the dough together; trim off the excess pastry which can be used as decorations and to form a round knob for the top (as on the lid of a tureen), attached with egg white. Lay a narrow strip of dough round the edge of the pasty to reinforce it; brush the top with egg yolk and bake in preheated oven (400°F./Gas mark 6) until golden. Allow pasty to cool, then, with a sharp knife, cut out a round 'lid'. Lift up lid and carefully remove napkin.

Prepare meat filling as for Meat Balls recipe (p. 50). Make a sauce with the butter, flour, wine and stock, and mix half with the meat, serving the rest separately. Fill pasty shortly before serving, and replace lid.

Tripe with Tomato Sauce *Kutteln nach Schaffhauser Art*

The tripe is usually bought parboiled.

1 lb. 2 oz. tripe, cut in small pieces
2 tablespoons flour
1½ oz. butter or fat
2 onions
1 small tin tomato purée
caraway seeds
nutmeg
pepper
paprika
1 wine glass white wine
10 fl. oz. beef stock
little cream
lemon juice

Sprinkle the tripe with flour and fry lightly, together with the chopped onions. Add tomato purée and spices; pour in wine and stock, and if necessary, a little water, until the tripe is just covered. Simmer 45 minutes, stirring occasionally. Finally add little lemon juice and cream. Serve with boiled or fried potatoes.

Veal Schnitzel 'Cordon Bleu' *Kalbsschnitzel Cordon Bleu*

This particular schnitzel, or escalope, despite its part-French, part-German name, is also closely related to the Italian Papagallo.

Per person:

1 double schnitzel (cutlet)
salt
pepper
lemon juice
1 slice bacon
1 slice Gruyère cheese
flour
1 egg
breadcrumbs
butter or fat

Ask the butcher to cut the veal cutlet with his sharp knife in such a way that the two slices still hang together at the back like the pages of a book. Rub the outside with salt, pepper and lemon juice, and between the 'pages' place the slice of cheese and slice of bacon, both slightly smaller than the cutlet. Firmly press both halves of the stuffed cutlet together and roll first in flour, then in beaten egg and finally in breadcrumbs. Fry the veal in hot fat, on both sides, for about 10 minutes and serve with vegetables or salad.

Emmenthal Veal Schnitzel *Emmentaler Schnitzel*

4 well-beaten veal schnitzel (cutlets)
salt
pepper
4 slices Gruyère cheese, cut to same size as the schnitzel
lemon juice
flour
1 egg
breadcrumbs
2½ oz. butter
1 dessertspoon grated cheese

Sprinkle cutlets with lemon juice, salt, pepper and a little grated cheese. Leave for 5 minutes, then roll in flour, beaten egg and breadcrumbs, and fry on one side in hot butter. Turn, reduce heat, place on fried side of each cutlet a slice of Gruyère cheese and very slowly fry the other side. Serve with crisp salad.

Stuffed Calf's Heart *Gefülltes Kalbsherz*

1 calf's heart
1 onion
2 oz. butter
salt
pepper
little flour
little milk
3½ fl. oz. sour cream

For the marinade:

2½ fl. oz. wine vinegar
2½ fl. oz. water
good ½ pint white wine
1 bay leaf
1 onion
peppercorns
cloves

For the stuffing:

3¾ oz. minced veal
1¼ oz. cooked ham
1 tablespoon breadcrumbs
1 egg
parsley
marjoram

Cut heart open and remove skin and gristle. Bring wine, vinegar, water and spices to the boil and allow to get cold, then add the heart and leave to marinade.

Chop ham and mix with other ingredients for the stuffing. Dry the heart, stuff it and sew up the opening. Fry heart, with the sliced onion, on all sides until brown. Pour in boiling water and part of the marinade liquid, and cook slowly in covered saucepan for at least 1 hour. Then remove the heart, cut in thick slices and keep hot.

Stir a little flour into the milk, add the rest of the cooking liquid and the sour cream, sieve this sauce, pour over the heart and serve with mashed potatoes.

Roast Chicken with Onions and Mushrooms

Güggeli oder Mistchratzerli

Both German names are dialect terms for a young chicken or cockerel. The recipe serves 10.

2 chickens (half chicken per person)
salt
5 fl. oz. cream
2½ fl. oz. beef stock
4 oz. diced bacon

pepper
3 oz. butter
$2\frac{1}{2}$ fl. oz. white wine
4 oz. button onions
8 oz. cooked mushrooms or 1 small tin chanterelles

Rub cleaned, washed and dried chickens with salt and pepper, and truss in the usual way. Roast chickens in butter in hot oven (425°F./Gas mark 7) for about 35 minutes, basting from time to time. Meanwhile boil onions, sauté mushrooms and lightly fry bacon. Keep hot. Remove chickens when done, pour off butter, add white wine to remains in the tin and bring to the boil. Add cream and stock, and when the sauce has thickened somewhat, strain through a sieve. Place the halved chickens on a preheated dish, garnish with onions and mushrooms and sprinkle over bacon. Serve with mashed potatoes or macaroni, and hand the sauce separately.

POPULAR SAUSAGE DISHES

Switzerland is proud of its great choice of sausages (see list p. 135) and of sausage dishes, of which just a few are given here. Cervela is probably the favourite, as will be seen from the German names of many dishes, but in these, as in the other recipes, sausages more easily obtainable taste every bit as good.

Znüni *Znüni*

sausages
small rolls

As a mid-morning snack, cold sausages are combined with hot baked rolls (usually Bürli—half wheat, half rye).

Poor Man's Trout *Züri-Chrebs*

sausages
onions
little flour

Skin and halve the sausages, making a few cross-cuts on the outside. Fry onion rings in hot fat until yellow. Remove onions and fry sausages in same fat, on both sides. Add cooked onions, sprinkle with little flour, pour over 2 tablespoons water, heat through and serve.

Sausages on Skewers *Cervela am Spiess*

Make a cross-cut at one end of each sausage, not quite down to the middle. Spear the other end with a skewer and hold over flame until brown and crisp (good for barbecues).

Grilled Sausage *Cervela vom Grill*

sausages
cheese slices
bacon slices

Skin and halve sausages lengthways (preferably Knackwurst). Place a strip of cheese in the centre of each, wrap round with slice of bacon, secure with toothpick and grill on both sides.

Sausage Salad *Cervela-Salat*

Skin the cooked sausages (preferably Knackwurst) and slice thinly. Serve with a salad dressing of oil, vinegar, mustard and onions; garnish with gherkins.

Sausages with Onion Sauce *Bratwürste mit Zwiebelsauce*

Very much to a man's taste, these fried sausages are served with 'Bölleschweizi', i.e. plenty of fried onions in a thin gravy, accompanied by fried or mashed potatoes.

4 veal or pork sausages
milk
1 oz. butter
2 sliced onions
1 teaspoon flour
10 fl. oz. beef stock

Soak the sausages in milk before frying—they are then less likely to burst. Grease frying pan with butter, place sausages side by side in pan and let them fry quite slowly in their own fat until brown on both sides. A little more butter is needed for veal sausages since they are less greasy. Keep sausages hot and fry onion rings in the same fat until golden-brown. Arrange rings on the sausages and fry the flour—still in the same fat—till lightly browned. Add stock and allow to thicken, then pour the gravy over the sausages and onions.

Pork Sausages Cooked in Wine *Waadtländer Bratwurst*

1 lb. 2 oz. pork sausages for frying
10 fl. oz. white wine
10 fl. oz. beef stock

Pour the wine into a frying pan. Arrange the sausages in a flat coil and place in the pan. Pierce with a fork and place pan on heat. Let the wine boil away, when the sausages will start to fry in their own fat. Turn when fried on one side. When brown both sides, remove sausages to a warm plate. Pour stock into the pan and scrape up any bits that remain. Allow this gravy to boil for a moment, and serve with the sausages.

Leek and Sausage Stew *Lauchgemüse mit Wurst*
[Canton Waadt]

You may sample this stew from Lausanne to Montreux. It is made with a special kind of sausage, or rather two different kinds, the *saucisse au choux* and the *saucisse au foie*, both smoked sausages, with cabbage and liver respectively included in the fillings. Ordinary sausages can be equally well used. This serves 8.

2¼ lb. leeks
½ oz. flour
1¼ oz. butter
salt
pepper
1 lb. 2 oz. potatoes
2 large sausages, or 8 oz. pork sausages

Cut leeks in finger-length pieces and blanch for 5 minutes in lightly salted boiling water. Make a white sauce with the flour, butter and 1 pint of the water used to blanch the leeks. Season. Cook leeks and raw potatoes, cut in pieces, slowly in the sauce for 20 minutes, covering the saucepan. Then add the sausages and leave to simmer very gently for another 15 minutes. Cut sausages into thick slices at the table.

Meat Balls *Bratkügeli*

These are made from sausage meat bought loose by weight, which can also be mixed with other minced meat.

1 lb. 2 oz. beef sausage meat
1 onion stuck with cloves
1 tablespoon fat
¾ oz. flour
3 dessertspoons cream
1 wine glass white wine (optional)
8 oz. mushrooms (optional)

Heat saucepan of lightly salted water, add onion and allow to simmer. Using a wet spoon, divide sausage meat into small balls, add to the saucepan of water and allow to simmer very gently for 10 minutes. Fry flour in fat until just yellow, add few spoonfuls of the cooking water, the cream and, if desired, a glass of white wine. Drain Meat Balls, add to sauce and let them simmer for a few minutes before serving (with mushrooms if wished). Delicious with noodles.

Sausage Meat with Onions *Adrio*

large piece of caul, pig's or calf's
1 lb. 2 oz. beef sausage meat
parsley
2 oz. butter
1 large sliced onion

Wash and dry the caul and cut in small pieces of equal size. On each piece, place sprig of parsley and 3 tablespoons sausage meat. Fold over edges to make small flat 'parcels'. Fry parcels in hot butter on both sides till golden-brown, then leave pan on very low heat for at least 30 minutes. Remove and keep hot; fry onion rings in the same fat till lightly browned, add little water to make gravy and serve with the meat.

POTATOES COOKED IN MANY WAYS

Coffee and Fried Potatoes

There are some ways with potatoes which are now equally at home wherever potatoes are eaten: potatoes in their jackets, boiled potatoes, *pommes frites*, chips, mashed potatoes, potato salad, potato soup. In addition, each country has, of course, its own special dishes; and in Switzerland, first and foremost comes 'Rösti', closely followed by a great many other nourishing, tasty and original recipes, well deserving a chapter to themselves.

SWISS FRIED POTATOES—THE FAMOUS RÖSTI

There is a popular story of the Swiss who goes to London or New York, orders Rösti the very first thing and is thoroughly indignant when he finds that people do not even know what he is talking about. In fact, the genuine Rösti, Bernese Rösti, are truly delicious. The Emmenthal farmers like nothing better than a large plate of nourishing Rösti in the morning before they go to work, accompanied by white coffee (half and half). Rösti with salad, and milky coffee, make a satisfying supper for children; though they are usually served in restaurants, and otherwise at home, with sausages or meat.

Rösti *Rösti*

1¾ lb. potatoes (a firm variety), boiled in the jackets the day before
3 oz. butter or lard or fat
salt
1½ tablespoons water or milk

Peel and slice potatoes, and cut into thin strips. Heat large frying pan, and let the fat get hot; then put in the potatoes, sprinkle with salt and fry, turning them constantly. When potatoes have soaked up the fat—some varieties take more than others—add more fat. Now form a kind of 'cake' by pushing the potatoes from the edges of the pan towards the middle and flattening the top. Sprinkle with a little water or milk, reduce heat and cover with a lid or inverted dish which exactly fits the pan. Shake covered pan occasionally to prevent potatoes burning and leave on low heat for at least 15 minutes. The potatoes must stick together, but not to the bottom of the pan. When cooked, invert the frying pan and turn Rösti into the lid. Slide potatoes from the lid on to a plate, with golden-brown side now on top.

Popular Rösti Variants *Beliebte Rösti Varianten*

1. Sauté approx. 2 tablespoons chopped onions in fat before placing potatoes in the pan. The onions should not be allowed to brown. In this case, potatoes need less fat.
2. Sauté 2–3½ oz. diced bacon before adding potatoes. Go easy on the salt!
3. Just before potatoes are done, sprinkle with 3 dessertspoons grated Gruyère cheese and continue frying for a few more minutes.
4. Sprinkle cooked potatoes with grated, fragrant herb cheese before serving.
5. Make Rösti with raw potatoes. Grate potatoes finely, then proceed as above. Fry 10 minutes extra.

Fribourg Fried Potatoes *Freiburger Kartoffeln*

These are distant relatives of the Bernese Rösti—but of course Fribourg is only half an hour's train journey from Bern.

2¼ lb. potatoes
salt
2½ oz. butter
2 eggs
2 oz. grated cheese
10 fl. oz. milk
nutmeg

Peel the uncooked potatoes and cut in approx. ⅛-inch slices. Dry the slices, sprinkle with salt and fry first uncovered, then with lid on the pan, until soft. Meanwhile mix eggs, cheese and milk, add nutmeg and pour the mixture over the potatoes. Cover the pan again and leave for 10 minutes on low heat, shaking frequently. Turn the potato 'cake' on to a warm plate with the golden-brown crust on top.

Cheese-baked Potatoes *Tessiner Kartoffeln*

8 large oval potatoes
salt
butter or oil
3¾ oz. grated cheese

Peel potatoes and make four cross-cuts in each without cutting through—so that the slices hold together at the bottom. Place potatoes on greased baking sheet, sprinkle with salt, brush with oil or melted butter and bake in hot oven for about 45 minutes (400°F./Gas mark 6). Then sprinkle with cheese, seeing that some penetrates between the slices, again baste with little butter and replace in the oven for another 10 minutes, till a golden crust has formed.

Potatoes in Brown Sauce *Saucen-Gummeli*
[Canton Schweiz]

Despite the strange Swiss name, this is another tasty potato dish. The brown sauce has a piquant flavour due to the addition of vinegar.

2¼ lb. potatoes
2 dessertspoons fat
1½ oz. flour
salt
1 large onion
1–2 dessertspoons vinegar
2 cloves
1 bay leaf
1 pint water or stock
chopped parsley
chopped chives

Peel potatoes and cut them in approx. ⅜-inch-thick slices. Fry the chopped onion in the fat, add raw potato slices, sprinkle with flour and salt and pour in 1 pint water or stock. Finally add spices, herbs and vinegar, and cook for about 35 minutes, or till done.

Sauté Potato Crumbs *Maluns*
[Graubünden]

The canton of Graubünden has contributed to the Swiss Confederation not only a specific language, Romansh, but also a number of well-known culinary specialities, among which the air-dried Bündner meat is the most famous. Maluns is an old Bündner dish which is still frequently served, with large quantities of white coffee.

8 oz. grated boiled potatoes
8 oz. thinly sliced boiled potatoes
8 oz. plain flour
salt
5 oz. lard
2 oz. unsalted butter

Mix grated and sliced potatoes with the flour and salt, while a tablespoon of lard melts in a large frying pan. Add potatoes to the fat and keep turning them, adding a little more lard at regular intervals. After about 40 minutes they form small, light-brown potato 'crumbs', which must remain soft. Finally add butter and serve.

Apple, Potato and Bacon Stew *'s Köch*
[Canton Glarus]

This is one of many stews made from potatoes, apples and smoked meat.

10 rashers bacon
10 sweet apples (dried apples can be used)
piece of smoked or fresh pork
2¼ lb. potatoes
1 pint water

Cover the bottom of a casserole or saucepan with the bacon, arrange the halved, cored but unpeeled apples on top, then the meat and the potatoes. Add water, cover with a tight-fitting lid and cook for 1–1½ hours, or until meat is tender, in the oven (355°F./Gas mark 4) or on very low heat.

Potato Dumplings *Kartoffelpfluten*

1¼ lb. peeled cooked potatoes
1 egg
salt
pepper
8 fl. oz. milk
4 oz. grated cheese
little fat
2½ oz. butter
1 onion
1 tablespoon breadcrumbs

Rub the hot potatoes through a sieve and mix with egg, seasoning, hot milk and 2 oz. grated cheese to a smooth paste. Melt little fat, dip two spoons first in the fat and then in the potato mixture to form dumplings, which should be placed on hot plate and sprinkled with the rest of the cheese. Lightly brown the butter, fry the onion rings with the breadcrumbs and pour sizzling over the dumplings.

Small Potato Dumplings *Pizokel*
[Graubünden/Lower Engadine]

These small dumplings are made from uncooked potatoes.

3 medium-sized peeled potatoes
8 oz. plain flour
2 eggs.
8 fl. oz. milk (or half milk, half water)
salt
2 oz. butter
grated cheese (optional)
breadcrumbs (optional)
1 onion (optional)

Mix milk, eggs, grated raw potatoes, flour and a little salt to a thick paste and leave for about 1 hour. Bring salted water to boil in a large saucepan. Spread paste on a wooden board, cut off pieces and turn into the water. As the dumplings appear on the surface, take them out with a perforated spoon, rinse with cold water and let them drain. When all the paste has been used, fry dumplings in butter until crisp and brown. Or put them back into the simmering water, leave for 2 minutes, drain and turn on to a dish; then sprinkle with grated cheese and pour over melted brown butter, with breadcrumbs and onion rings browned in the butter, if liked.

Baked Potato Purée *Ofentori*
[Canton Unterwalden]

Left-over mashed potatoes may also be used for this dish.

1½ lb. potatoes, peeled and sliced roughly
salt
1 egg
5 fl. oz. cream (or milk)
butter
4 oz. bacon, cut in thin strips

Boil potatoes in salted water; drain well and while still hot, rub through a sieve and mix to a smooth purée with cream and egg. Butter a fireproof dish. Fill with the purée and put strips of bacon throughout, but let them protrude a little way at the top. Bake in medium-hot oven (400°F./Gas mark 6).

Baked Potato Purée (2) *Ofenguck*
[Canton Zug]

A close relative of the preceding dish.

approx. 1½ lb. mashed potatoes
little fat
4 oz. diced bacon
4 oz. diced cheese

Grease a baking sheet or flan tin and coat to a thickness of about ½ inch with mashed potatoes. Make small depressions all over and fill these with pieces of cheese and bacon. Bake in hot oven (425°F./Gas mark 6) till lightly browned.

Bean and Potato Purée *Kartoffel- und Bohnenpüree*
[Tessin/Valley of Maggia]

Before the butcher from Locarno started visiting the villages with his van once or twice a week, it often happened in out of the way mountain valleys of the Tessin that people had to go without meat for weeks on end. This is a recipe they would have when no meat was available. It can be served as a main dish, but try it also with small mutton chops or frying sausages. It serves 8.

1 lb. 2 oz. potatoes
1 lb. 2 oz. French beans
2–3 oz. butter
salt

chopped fresh herbs (parsley, mint, basil, marjoram)
pepper

Peel and slice the potatoes, and boil together with the beans in salted water. Drain well, pass through a sieve or mincer and mix with butter (cut in pieces) and chopped herbs, and seasoning. The green-flecked purée has a particularly delicious aroma.

Potato-Pitte *Kartoffel-Pitte*

[Graubünden]

This makes a savoury accompaniment to coffee, can be served with salad for supper, or as a snack at any time. The recipe serves 8.

2¼ lb. potatoes
7½ oz. dried pears
1 egg
2½ oz. butter
7½ oz. flour
10 fl. oz. warm milk
4 oz. diced bacon
salt
pepper

Peel and grate the raw potatoes, press to extract any liquid and pour it away. The dried pears must be soaked beforehand. Slice them thinly. Mix all ingredients except bacon with the warm milk and melted butter to a dough, and lay over greased, edged baking sheet. Sprinkle the top with bacon and bake in medium-hot oven (400°F./Gas mark 6) for 30 minutes.

Potato, Meat and Tomato Pie *Kartoffel-Tomaten Torte*

[Tessin]

5½ oz. minced beef
2 oz. butter
½ onion
clove of garlic, chopped
chopped parsley
1 lb. 2 oz. raw potatoes
3 tablespoons oil
breadcrumbs
1 tin peeled tomatoes
approx. 5 fl. oz. beef stock

Melt 1 oz. butter in pan and add minced meat, parsley, chopped onion and garlic. Fry gently together for 2–3 minutes, turning frequently, then remove and put aside. Peel the potatoes, and slice thinly or shred; fry in the oil. Grease small pie dish and sprinkle with breadcrumbs. Fill with alternate layers of potato, meat and tomato. The top layer should be potato. Pour over the juice from the tin of tomatoes and some of the stock, sprinkle with breadcrumbs lightly, dot surface with butter. Bake in hot oven (425°F./Gas mark 7) for 15–20 minutes.

PASTA, RICE, DUMPLINGS AND CEREALS

Taking Millet to Strasbourg

The following recipes represent only a few examples of an endless variety. It would be a fascinating study to investigate the culinary influences from neighbouring countries that have penetrated Switzerland through the centuries, particularly in the sphere of cereal dishes, where the many Swiss variations have been gradually replaced by Italian pasta and rice or South German and Austrian dumplings and balls—to mention just a few.

Various kinds of pasta have become firm favourites in the Swiss kitchen, not only in the Tessin but equally in German-speaking Switzerland (though less perhaps in western Switzerland which tends more towards French cooking). There are several factories in Switzerland which produce an astonishing variety of shapes and forms of excellent quality; and German-Swiss housewives on their frequent journeys across the St Gotthard Pass have long since learnt to prepare pasta in the Italian manner, *al dente*, and not to overcook it. Nowhere outside Italy does one find better 'Spaghetti à la Napolitaine' (with tomato sauce), 'Spaghetti à la Bolognese' (with a sauce of minced meat, tomatoes and wine), or 'Piccata à la Milanaise' (spaghetti with fresh butter and cheese and served with tiny veal slices). Fresh Ravioli and Cappelletti filled with meat can be bought in many shops.

Besides the recipes adopted from Italy, the German-Swiss have their own ways with pasta and love to smother their noodles in grated cheese, fried onion rings and melted butter, the traditional Swiss garnishes. But the traditional forerunners of modern factory-made noodles etc. are not in fact the home-made kind but,

throughout German Switzerland, the varieties of small dumplings known as 'Knöpfli' and 'Spätzli'.

Dumplings *Knöpfli und Spätzli*

The word Spätzli means 'little sparrows', whereas Knöpfli are 'little buttons'—but the basic mixture is the same for both. For Spätzli, the dough is spread on a wooden board and thin strips are cut and thrown into a pan of boiling salted water. Knöpfli are normally made by pressing the dough through a special sieve.

14 oz. plain flour
3 eggs
good ¼ pint water
1 teaspoon salt
butter
breadcrumbs (optional)
onions (optional)
grated cheese

Sieve flour and blend in the eggs, water and salt to a smooth paste. Cover and leave for 30 minutes. Cut strips and throw them into boiling water, as described for Small Potato Dumplings on p. 56, not all together but one at a time. As each comes to the surface, remove with a perforated spoon and drain. Arrange on preheated dish, pour over brown butter, and fried onions or fried breadcrumbs if liked. Sprinkle with grated cheese, and serve with salad, or with stewed apples.

Spinach Dumplings *Spinat-Spätzli*

Add 2 tablespoons finely chopped spinach to the basic dough and proceed as above.

Liver Dumplings *Leber-Spätzli*

Add $3\frac{3}{4}$ oz. finely chopped liver to the basic dough and proceed as above.

Fried Dumplings *Aufgebackene Spätzli*

Fry any left-over dumplings in butter and, just before serving, pour over an egg sauce (e.g. rich Béchamel sauce with chopped hard-boiled egg added).

Potato Dumplings (see p. 56)

Potatoes and Pasta *Kartoffel und Teigwaren*
[Canton Glarus]

Not beneficial to vital statistics, but very suitable for hungry boys!

7 oz. noodles or other pasta
9 oz. potatoes
salt
$3\frac{3}{4}$ oz. (herb) cheese
2 oz. butter or fat
1 oz. breadcrumbs or
2 dessertspoons onion rings

Peel and cube potatoes and cook with the noodles in salted water or, if you are not quite sure how long each will take (it depends on the variety of pasta, the size of the potato cubes and the kind of potato used), cook separately. The potatoes should be firm when cooked, and not broken. Reheat both quickly in boiling water if necessary, and drain well. Alternate layers of pasta etc. with layers of grated cheese in a deep dish, and pour over the sizzling brown butter with onion rings or breadcrumbs fried in it. Serve with salad, or for a change, with tart apple sauce.

Spinach Rolls *Krautkapaunen*
[Graubünden]

There are many recipes for this nourishing dish. The following comes from Surselva. It serves 12.

$5\frac{1}{2}$ oz. diced lean bacon or cooked meat
4 oz. diced white bread
3 eggs
5 fl. oz. liquid (half milk, half water)

1 large chopped onion
chopped herbs (parsley, chives, rosemary, basil)
2 oz. butter or fat
10 oz. plain flour
salt
3¾ oz. currants
40 large spinach leaves
grated cheese
2 oz. unsalted butter

Lightly cook bacon, bread, onion and herbs in the fat and allow to cool. Make a fairly firm batter with the flour, milk and water, eggs and salt, and stir in the cold bacon etc. and the currants. Dip spinach leaves quickly in boiling water; drain and roll up each one with dessertspoon of the mixture in the middle. Tie with thin string. Let these rolls simmer very gently for about 20 minutes in salted water. Drain carefully. Sprinkle with plenty of grated cheese and pour over brown butter.

A little spinach may be worked into the filling itself if liked, and the currants may be omitted.

Risotto *Risotto*

The people of the Tessin, like the Italians, eat Risotto in place of soup. Risotto is also popular throughout Switzerland with meat, or as a supper dish with salad. In the Tessin, Risotto is prepared in the Italian way, the rice fried with chopped onions in butter or oil, or in a mixture of half butter, half beef dripping, and the liquid added gradually as necessary. Elsewhere in Switzerland all the liquid is added at once, so that the rice swells slowly and is lighter, with the grains more separate.

10 oz. rice (round-grained variety)
2 oz. butter or oil (or half butter, half beef dripping)
1 small onion
10 fl. oz. dry white wine
1¾ pints beef stock
2 oz. grated Parmesan cheese

Tessin Method:

Do not wash rice, but rub in clean cloth and pick out any black grains. Skin and quarter the onion and fry in fat until tender. Remove onion and in the same fat fry the rice, stirring until pale golden. Pour in white wine and slowly add boiling stock until rice is barely covered. Cook without covering the pan. After

16–18 minutes, the rice should have absorbed the liquid and the grains should be soft. Fold in grated cheese with a fork, remove pan from the heat and leave, covered, for 3 minutes. Then serve at once.

Alternative Swiss Method:

Fry finely chopped onion and the rice in hot fat until rice appears translucent, but not golden. Pour in all the liquid and leave rice on low heat, covered, to steam rather than boil for 18 minutes. Then mix in the cheese, or pour it over the rice at table.

Variations on basic Risotto recipes:

1. Mix rice prepared as above with cooked mushrooms.
2. Fry chopped vegetables (carrots, celery, leek, peas, beans, tomatoes), as well as onions, with the rice.
3. Add chopped ham or salami to prepared rice.
4. Dissolve little saffron in approx. 5 fl. oz. of the beef stock and add with rest of liquid to the rice, to give it a golden colour.

Cabbage and Rice *Urner Kraut mit Reis*

2 onions
2 oz. fat
12 oz. rice
1¼ pints beef stock (made with stock cubes)
1 onion
salt
approx. 1¾-lb. savoy cabbage
2 oz. cheese
spoonful of butter

Chop and lightly brown 1 onion in fat and add rice. When rice is translucent, add the stock and cook till tender. Cut cabbage roughly in strips and cook separately until soft; then mix cabbage and cheese with the cooked rice. Season. Fry remaining onion in butter till lightly browned and pour sizzling over the rice etc. Thinly sliced leeks, instead of cabbage, can also be used.

Polenta *Polenta*

[Graubünden and Tessin]

'Polenta' is best described as a kind of maize porridge and is something of an acquired taste. In the Tessin maize is primarily eaten in the form of this thick 'porridge' which, the next day, is fried in slices. In Graubünden there are at least two or three dozen specialities made from maize, including soup, cakes, pies, bread with raisins, dumplings and, of course, Polenta made with water, milk or cream and served with a variety of garnishes.

9 oz. maize flour (or semolina)
2½ pints salted water

Bring water to the boil and add the maize. After a few minutes, start to fold the mixture with a wooden spoon continually, without stirring too much. Reduce heat and continue to fold, so that the Polenta neither sticks nor dries up, until cooked, smooth and soft. Considerable patience is needed (though there are also several kinds of instant Polenta which are sometimes obtainable and take only 3 minutes to prepare).

Polenta is served with stews of all kinds, goulash, fried liver or kidneys, roast pork or sausages; or simply with cheese poured over it, or sugar and cinnamon, and stewed apples.

Fried or Baked Polenta *Aufgebackene Polenta-Schnitten*

Polenta (prepared as above)
butter
grated cheese (for baking)
2 eggs (for baking)

Prepare Polenta according to the recipe above and while still hot, spread mixture on a flat china dish previously rinsed in cold water. Next day, cut the cold Polenta in strips or slices, or stamp out round shapes with the rim of a tumbler, and fry these in butter on both sides until lightly browned.

Serve with stewed apples, or salad. To bake, arrange slices of cold Polenta on greased baking sheet. Sprinkle with grated cheese and dot with butter, put a second layer of Polenta, cheese and butter on top, pour over 2 beaten eggs and bake in the oven for 20 minutes (400°F./Gas mark 6).

Fried Maize *Türkenribel*

14 oz. maize flour (or semolina)
1 pint boiling water
salt
3 oz. butter or fat
hot milk (if necessary)

Gradually blend boiling salted water with the maize flour or semolina or, if desired, a mixture of plain flour and maize flour. The maize should be moist but not lumpy. Cover and leave overnight in a warm place. Fry the maize in an iron pan with half the butter, turning it constantly and gradually adding more fat until small dry lumps begin to cake together (this takes at least 40 minutes). Should the maize become too dry, add a cup of hot milk, which should be completely absorbed. Serve with white coffee or stewed fruit.

Savoury Pudding *Plain in Pigna*
[Graubünden]

This is a kind of savoury pudding, for which a variety of left-overs may be used, according to what is available. Cold roast meat, diced bacon, salami or ham, raw or boiled potatoes, flour, semolina, sultanas, fat and cream or milk are combined—the variations are up to the cook. One example is given below. The same name also describes a dish made with sliced boiled, and then lightly fried, potatoes which are arranged on a baking sheet and covered with a thin pancake batter, and baked as a sort of cake in the oven.

3 oz. butter or fat
3 tablespoons plain flour
2 tablespoons maize flour
1 tablespoon semolina
3 diced raw potatoes
spoonful of chopped bacon
spoonful of diced ham or salami
spoonful of sultanas
salt
milk

Melt the fat and mix with all other ingredients, adding enough milk to make a thick paste. Grease shallow form or dish thoroughly and spread mixture on it to a thickness of about 2½ inches. Bake in the oven for about 40 minutes (400°F./Gas mark 6).

Fried Millet *Hirsotto*

In former times, millet porridge was also a staple food. Even today children learn in history lessons of the 'Millet Journeys' undertaken by the people of Zürich in 1456 and 1576. The aldermen of

Zürich carried hot millet in an iron pot to Strasbourg (the journey took nineteen hours) and solemnly proclaimed during the banquet which followed that the people of Zürich would come to the aid of their friends in Strasbourg, if need be, before the millet cooled in the pot.

Rice, potatoes and bread gradually ousted millet from its previous position; but during the Second World War, when rice was scarce, millet was recalled to favour and Risotto replaced with 'Hirsotto' (from the German word *Hirse* for millet). It has remained popular, particularly in view of its nutritional value (it is rich in important silicic acid).

10 oz. millet (usually available from health stores)
2 chopped onions
1½ oz. butter, or fat or oil
1½ pints meat or vegetable stock
1½ oz. unsalted butter
2 oz. grated cheese

Sauté the onions in hot fat until half cooked, add millet and fry for some minutes, stirring constantly. Pour in hot stock and cook for 14–18 minutes. Fold in unsalted butter and grated cheese, allow to stand for a few minutes in covered pan, then serve.

Semolina Balls *Griess-Pfluten*

1¼ pints milk
1 pint water
salt
5½ oz. semolina
2 oz. butter
2 tablespoons breadcrumbs
grated cheese to taste

Bring to the boil milk, water and little salt, and add semolina. Cook for 15 minutes, stirring occasionally, till the mixture has the consistency of thick porridge. Heat butter in small pan, dip a tablespoon in the butter and use it to take and form balls from the mixture. Arrange on dish, fry breadcrumbs in remaining butter and pour over. Sprinkle with grated cheese according to taste.

BREAD ... WITH BUTTER, EGGS AND MILK

On a visit to one of the bigger farms in Switzerland, you can still watch the farmer's wife baking enormous loaves of bread in a wood-fire oven, following the same recipe for the local type of bread that her mother, grandmother and great-grandmother used before her. The different sorts of bread and rolls sold in a baker's shop in Zürich, or any other Swiss city, are legion. Since the Second World War the desire for variety has strikingly increased; and a more than ample choice is supplied by the different kinds of bread from different regions, the types adopted or modified from those of neighbouring countries, bread made from wholemeal and other types of flour, and small rolls to suit every taste. For the interest of visitors from abroad, some of the names and specialities are listed on p. 136 Some of the richest and most delicious loaves are the 'Butterwecken'; and the yeast plaits described below are one of the best-known kinds.

Yeast Plait *Züpfe*

[Canton Bern]

These golden-brown loaves, temptingly displayed at the baker's, are thick at one end and taper towards the other.

1 lb. 2 oz. plain flour
1 teaspoon salt
3 oz. butter
10 fl. oz. milk

¼ oz. yeast
1 teaspoon sugar
2 eggs

Sift the warmed flour with the salt into a warm mixing bowl. Crumble the yeast and mix with teaspoon of sugar. After a few minutes, the yeast becomes liquid. Make a small depression in the flour and pour in the yeast. Melt butter slowly in small saucepan, add milk, and when mixture is barely lukewarm add it to the flour, together with 1 egg. Mix well together, knead and beat the dough until smooth and elastic. Leave covered in a warm place for about 1½ hours.

Place dough on a board and form two long rolls of equal size, both thick in the middle and thin at the ends. Place these crosswise one over the other and plait into a four-part twist. Since the rolls of dough are thickest in the middle, the plait will automatically take a pointed shape. Place finished plait on a baking sheet, cover, and again leave for a while in a warm place. Brush with beaten egg, and bake in hot oven (425°F./Gas mark 7) for 40 minutes or longer. The loaf is done if, when tested with a knitting needle, the needle comes out dry.

WAYS WITH STALE BREAD

Swiss women have always been particularly inventive in the uses they make of bread in the kitchen. On widely scattered farms, where neither butcher nor greengrocer is near by, bread still serves, together with the ever-plentiful eggs, milk and butter, in numerous novel ways. Everyone crumbles bread into a cup of milk or milky coffee and spoons it out. Then there are Bread Soup (p. 3) and the many ways of serving bread and cheese (p. 16,19). 'Fotzelschnitten' are slices of bread soaked in milk, dipped in beaten egg and fried in deep fat until golden-brown, then sprinkled with sugar and cinnamon. 'Schiterbig' consists of thin strips of bread prepared as above with milk and beaten egg, then fried, and finally heaped on a dish and covered with a thick vanilla sauce. Here are further examples of a rich variety.

Bread Fritters *Vogelheu*

A popular evening meal, especially with children.

bread, thinly sliced or cubed
3¾ oz. butter
4 eggs
5 fl. oz. milk
salt

Fry the bread in hot butter in a large pan until golden. If bread is stale, pour over little boiling milk beforehand and leave for a few minutes before frying. Mix milk and salt with the eggs, as for scrambled egg. Pour mixture over the bread and keep turning slices in pan until all liquid has been absorbed. Serve with salad, or stewed fruit.

Fried Apples *Apfelrösti*

Again, very popular with children and a good way of using up stale bread. This recipe serves 6.

2¼ lb. apples
9 oz. bread (white, brown or dark)
4¾ oz. butter
5½ oz. sugar
2½ fl. oz. water

Cut peeled apples in thin slices. Bring to the boil with the sugar and water, then leave to simmer for a minute or two. Cut bread in thin slices and fry in butter until golden; add apples, mix well together and cook until apples are tender.

Tin Cake *Matafan*

[Fribourg]

14 oz. plain white bread (it can well be stale)
1¼ pints milk
little salt
2–3 eggs
2 oz. sugar
1 tablespoon oil
5½ oz. plain flour
2 oz. butter
sugar for sprinkling

Cut bread in finger-thick slices. Pour over boiling milk and leave bread to soak for a few minutes. Drain slices of bread and place side by side on greased baking sheet. Stir together the flour, milk, eggs, oil, salt and sugar to a smooth pancake batter. Pour over the bread and dot with butter on top. Bake in medium-hot oven (380°F./Gas mark 5) for 30 minutes until golden. Cut in pieces, sprinkle with sugar and serve with apple sauce or stewed fruit.

MILK DISHES

Fenz *Fenz*

Fenz is almost a legend, a kind of primeval dish prepared by the cowherds who spend the summer on the alp or mountain pastures and, apart from the flour which they take with them, live exclusively on the milk of their cows and milk products. On Sundays and feast days, 'Fenz' is the traditional dish, made from butter, new milk and flour. Recipes vary from alp to alp and from mountain to mountain but the following is typical.

10 oz. butter
1¼ pints whey or milk
10 oz. plain flour
salt

Melt butter and when it starts to foam lightly, sprinkle in the flour. Fry till just yellow, then pour in the whey or boiling milk. Salt well and stir for 15 minutes. When the butter fat floats on the surface, the mixture is ready to be turned into bowls. At home, Fenz is best prepared over a spirit cooker in a fondue pan or any enamelled saucepan.

Poltö *Poltö*

A similar dish from the Tessin, for which, however, no butter is used. Stir 7½ oz. plain flour into 1¼ pints milk, add 1 pint cream, salt, and bring mixture to the boil. Stir for 20 minutes. The Poltö should have the consistency of an omelette.

Milk Pudding *Plattenmüesli*

The simplest of all milk-and-egg dishes and popular with children.

5 eggs
1¼ pints milk
2 oz. sugar
pinch of salt
grated rind of 1 lemon
little flour

Mix eggs, sugar, milk, salt and lemon rind thoroughly. Grease and dust with flour a shallow pie dish, pour in mixture and bake in the oven (380°F./Gas mark 5) for 30 minutes until golden.

Since eggs are not as cheap as they used to be, this dish may also be prepared in the following way. First cook milk with cornflour, semolina or rice, to a porridge consistency. Allow to cool slightly, then stir in 2 eggs, with sugar, salt and lemon rind, and bake in the oven as above.

OMELETTES, PANCAKES AND BATTERS

In Switzerland, the word 'omelette' has two meanings. In the French-speaking region (and in most hotels and restaurants of German-speaking Switzerland), the term is used in the French sense. But elsewhere, when the Swiss housewife says 'omelette' she means the French *crêpes* or pancakes. Here is a well-tried recipe for the batter.

Basic Pancake Batter *Omelettenteig*

10 oz. plain flour
15 fl. oz. liquid (half milk, half water)
3 large or 4 small eggs
1 tablespoon oil
salt
butter or oil for frying

Sift the flour into mixing bowl, add the liquid, eggs, salt and oil and mix quickly and thoroughly with an egg whisk until smooth. According to the type of flour, it may be necessary to add a little more liquid. If the pancakes are to be thick and airy, mix in the egg yolks only at first, beat the egg whites separately till stiff and fold in last of all. It is advisable to prepare the batter at least half an hour before cooking so as to allow the flour to swell. Fry pancakes on both sides in little butter or oil and keep warm in the oven in a fireproof dish. Serve with salad or stewed fruit, or fill with spinach, liver, kidneys, mushrooms or cheese. Left-overs can be rolled, cut in thin strips and added to soup.

Jura Omelette *Jura-Omelette*

[Canton Bern]

- 3 tablespoons diced bacon
- butter for frying
- 1 chopped onion
- 1 chopped tomato (or other vegetable)
- 3–4 boiled potatoes
- 3¾ oz. grated Emmenthal cheese
- salt
- pepper

Slowly fry bacon in frying pan, add chopped onion, then the diced potatoes and vegetables. When potatoes etc. are tender, mix eggs with the cheese and seasoning and pour over the vegetables. Finish as for an ordinary French omelette, fold over and serve.

Gingerbread Fingers *Bacheschnitte*

These were originally made from 'Biberfladen'—the large round, brown gingerbread which are a speciality of the canton of Appenzell. But why eat it just in that form? The Appenzell countrywomen cut gingerbread in narrow fingers, dip these in pancake batter and fry in deep fat. The fingers are sprinkled with sugar and cinnamon and served with coffee.

Pancake Rolls *Eierkutteln*

- ingredients as for pancake batter (p. 72)
- 2½ fl. oz. milk
- 2 oz. butter
- 2 oz. grated cheese (optional)

Prepare pancakes in the usual way. Roll up each one, cut in thin strips and arrange in a well-buttered dish. Pour over the milk, dot with butter and, if desired, sprinkle grated cheese on top, and bake in hot oven (425°F./Gas mark 7) for 20 minutes.

Cholermues *Cholermues*

[Canton Unterwalden]

Prepare pancake batter as above (p. 72), but use half milk, half cream, instead of milk and water. When one side of the pancake is cooked but the other still underdone, cut pancake in small shreds and continue to fry in butter until crisp and brown. Sprinkle with sugar and cinnamon, and serve.

Bernese Apple Pancakes *Berner Apfel-Omelette*

9 oz. plain flour
3 eggs
1 pint liquid (half milk, half water)
salt
2–3 tablespoons oil
4 large or 8 small ripe apples
fat for frying
sugar
cinnamon

Mix flour, eggs and liquid, salt and oil as for pancake batter (see p. 72). If necessary, add little more liquid—or little more flour—flour differs slightly in quality. Peel and core apples and slice thinly; add to the batter. Heat fat in frying pan and make rather thick pancakes. Cooking heat should not be too fierce, or the underside of the pancake will burn before the apples are done. When underside is golden-brown, turn pancake on to saucepan lid, add little more fat to pan, return pancake and cover and fry till second side is done. Sprinkle with sugar and cinnamon. Apple Pancakes must not be allowed to stand before serving.

Cherry Pancakes *Chriesi-Omelette*

Mix pancake batter (p. 72) with stoned cherries and fry as for Apple Pancakes above, but for a little longer.

Fried Apple Batter *Basler Pfnutli*

5 oz. plain flour
½–¾ pint white wine
2½ oz. sugar
salt
2 dessertspoons Kirsch
1 lb. 2 oz. tart apples
fat or butter
sugar
cinnamon (optional)

Stir the cold wine into the flour, add sugar, little salt, Kirsch and finely chopped apples. Leave to stand for 30 minutes. Heat butter or fat in frying pan, dip a large spoon first into the fat and then in the batter, and fry batter a spoonful at a time. Fry in plenty of fat on both sides until golden and serve sprinkled with sugar, and cinnamon if liked.

SWEET AND SAVOURY TARTS AND PASTIES

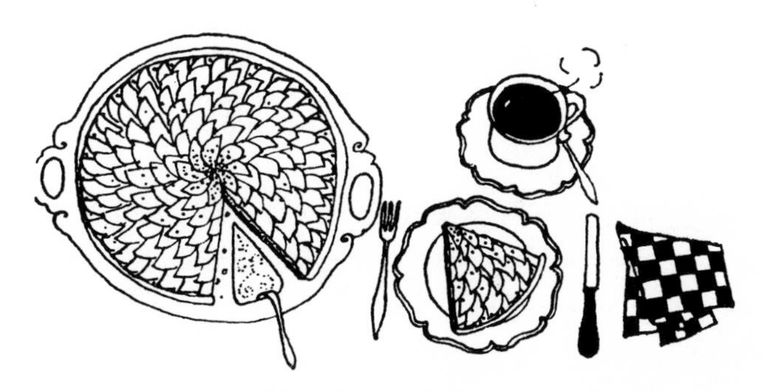

Apple Tart and Coffee

At lunch-time the bakery windows in Swiss cities are decorated with large round, open tarts filled with vegetables, cheese or fruit: these are the 'Wähen'. They are not just for dessert but, like the Italian pizza, which they resemble, are a meal in themselves, served with coffee or tea and, in winter, possibly preceded by hot soup. In former times, they were traditional washday fare, for which no cooking time on the day was needed. The Wähen are known by other names: the Schaffhausen 'Bölletünne' are onion tarts, and the Appenzell 'Kästönnele' are made with cheese.

Wähen can be made with either a yeast dough or medium short pastry. The yeast dough is usually preferred for savoury fillings—spinach, cheese, onion, bacon, etc., and the pastry for fruit fillings with or without sugar. Use a square or oblong baking sheet.

Yeast Dough *Hefeteig*

14 oz. plain flour (warm)
½ oz. yeast
1 teaspoon salt
3 oz. butter or fat
approx. 5 fl. oz. milk (or half milk, half water)

Blend all ingredients together and knead until smooth. Leave for short time in a warm place to rise. Roll out. Grease an edged baking sheet and lay dough over it.

Tart Pastry *Wähenteig*

14 oz. plain flour
1 teaspoon salt
4 oz. butter or fat
½ teaspoon baking powder
5 fl. oz. cold water

For a sweet pastry, for use with fruit, use only pinch of salt, add 3¾ oz. sugar and use milk instead of water. Mix all dry ingredients together on a cold surface, work in the butter and water to a dough.

Bacon Tart *Speckwähe*

ingredients for Yeast Dough (above)
7½ oz. finely diced bacon
1½ oz. butter
salt
caraway seeds

Prepare basic Yeast Dough (above). Sprinkle over the bacon, caraway seeds, salt; trickle over melted butter, and bake in a medium-hot oven (400°F./Gas mark 6) for 35 minutes.

Onion Tart *Zwiebelwähe*

ingredients for Yeast Dough (above)
approx. 1½ lb. onions
4 oz. finely diced bacon
1½ oz. butter
1½ oz. flour
10 fl. oz. cream or milk
2–3 eggs
caraway seeds or paprika (optional)

Mix ingredients for Yeast Dough. Gently cook onions and bacon in butter until almost tender, dust with flour, pour in part of the cream or milk, and allow to cool for a while. Then add eggs and rest of liquid, season. Roll out dough to finger thickness, place on baking sheet and allow to stand for a little. Pour over the onion mixture, sprinkle with caraway or paprika if liked, and bake in very hot oven (445°F./Gas mark 8) for 30–40 minutes. Serve hot.

Cream Tart *Nidelwähe*

ingredients for Yeast Dough (p. 76)
1½ oz. flour
1 pint cream
salt
nutmeg

Prepare dough and line baking sheet (p. 76). Beat all ingredients together with an egg whisk until lightly foaming. Spread over prepared dough and bake in hot oven (425°F./Gas mark 7) for about 30 minutes, until golden.

Spinach Tart *Spinatwähe*

3 tablespoons grated bread
chopped parsley
2 oz. butter
1–3 eggs
1 lb. 2 oz. spinach
few spoonfuls Béchamel sauce or cream (optional)
ingredients for Yeast Dough as above
4 oz. diced bacon

Fry the bread in butter until golden, add parsley and continue to fry for a moment longer. Mix in the egg and prepared spinach (left-overs may be used). For a richer filling, a few spoonfuls thick Béchamel sauce or cream and another 2 eggs may be added. Spread the mixture on prepared dough (p. 76), sprinkle with diced bacon and bake in hot oven (425°F./Gas mark 7) for about 35 minutes.

Apple Tart *Apfelwähe*

Tart Pastry (p. 72)
1½ lb. tart apples
1 egg yolk
sugar
cinnamon

Roll out the dough to approx. ⅛-inch thickness, lay over baking sheet with an edge all round. Peel, core and slice apples and arrange in concentric circles on the dough. Brush edges with egg yolk and bake 45 minutes in hot oven (425°F./Gas mark 7). After 30 minutes, sprinkle apples with sugar and when the tart is done, sprinkle with more sugar and cinnamon. Alternatively, brush the raw apples with melted butter, then mix together 2 eggs, 10 fl. oz. milk and 1¾ oz. sugar and pour over the apples, baking as before.

Plum or Apricot Tart *Zwetschenwähe, Aprikosenwähe*

These are prepared like the Apple Tart above, using either fresh, or dried and soaked, fruit. Remove stones from 2 lb. plums or apricots and place halved fruit cut side downwards on the dough. Sprinkle fruit with sugar, pour over the egg-and-milk mixture as for the Apple Tart above, and bake as before.

Rhubarb Tart *Rhabarberwähe*

Peel and dice 1½ lb. rhubarb and sprinkle over the dough prepared as for Apple Tart. Sprinkle with sugar. Bake 15 minutes (425°F./Gas mark 7), then sprinkle with sugar again and pour over the egg-and-milk mixture as above (see Apple Tart). Replace in oven and bake until done.

If the dough is sprinkled with breadcrumbs before the rhubarb is added, the juice will be prevented from soaking into it.

Cherry Tart *Kirschenwähe*

Stalk and wash 1½ lb. cherries. The stones are usually left in to prevent loss of juice. Arrange over dough prepared as for Apple Tart above, pour over egg-and-milk mixture and bake, as above.

Easter Cake *Osterfladen*

5½ oz. rice
1¾ pints milk
salt
1 lb. 2 oz. short pastry
5½ oz. peeled and grated almonds
4 eggs
7 oz. sugar
4 oz. seedless raisins
grated rind of 1 lemon

Cook rice slowly in lightly salted milk, so that it swells, then leave to cool. Roll out dough fairly thinly and line a large greased baking tin. Mix rice with egg yolks and other ingredients, finally fold in beaten egg whites and spread mixture on the dough. Bake 45 minutes in medium-hot oven (400°F./Gas mark 6) and sprinkle with sugar before serving.

Cheese Cake (see p. 17)

Flat Cakes (see p. 97)

SAUSAGE ROLLS AND PASTIES

As an accompaniment to a glass of wine or beer, for evening entertaining or a late-night snack, small sausage rolls and hot pasties are very popular in Switzerland. They also stand reheating well. Puff paste or unsweetened short pastry is used, or a 'mock' puff paste can be made very quickly with equal parts of butter, cottage cheese and flour.

There are several kinds of sausage rolls, with a filling of sausage meat, with or without ham, or one or two small sausages. Try both.

Sausage Rolls *Wurstweggen*

10 oz. puff pastry	6 oz. chopped ham
6 oz. sausage meat	1 egg

Roll out the dough to approx. $\frac{1}{8}$-inch thickness and cut into oblongs about 5–6 inches long and 4 inches wide. Mix together sausage meat and ham and place some of the mixture in the centre of each oblong. Fold over the edges, brush with egg white and press firmly together. Brush top with egg yolk, pierce here and there with a fork and bake in hot oven (425°F./Gas mark 7) for 30 minutes.

Frankfurter Rolls *Schaffhauser Schübling Weggen*

Boiling sausages are used for these and Frankfurters are best (in place of the original Schüblinge).

1 lb. 2 oz. shortcrust pastry
2 pairs sausages
1 egg

Stand the dough in a cool place. Roll out to approx. $\frac{1}{16}$-inch thickness and cut into four oblongs, each slightly bigger than the sausages. Plunge sausages into hot (not boiling) water, then skin carefully. Place each pair of sausages on an oblong of dough, brush edges with egg white, cover with a second oblong and press the edges together. Brush outside with egg yolk, pierce with fork and bake in medium-hot oven (400°F./Gas mark 6) for about 30 minutes, until crisp and brown.

Neuchâtel Liver Patties *Neuenburger Leberpastetchen*

10 oz. puff paste, or 'mock' puff paste (use equal parts flour, butter and cottage cheese)
9 oz. calf's liver
1 egg and 1 egg yolk
1 onion
1 oz. butter
2 tablespoons breadcrumbs
salt
pepper
marjoram
parsley
sage
1 egg for brushing
3 dessertspoons brandy

Prepare dough and keep in refrigerator before using. Roll out thinly and line small patty tins. Sauté chopped onion in butter with liver and mix chopped liver/onions with breadcrumbs, egg, egg yolk, herbs and seasoning. Fill tins half full with this mixture and cover with circles of pastry. Cut a small hole in each 'lid' to allow steam to escape. Press lids down firmly, brush with beaten egg and bake in hot oven (425°F./Gas mark 7) for 20–30 minutes. Pour few drops of brandy through the hole in the lid into each patty, and serve.

Onion and Bacon Squares *Böllewegge*

1½ lb. Yeast Dough (p. 76)
5 large chopped onions
2 oz. finely diced bacon
2 oz. melted butter
¾ oz. flour
10 fl. oz. cream or top of the milk
3 eggs
salt
1 egg white for brushing

Leave dough to rise. Roll out, cut into squares and again leave to rise. Mix other ingredients to a thick paste and spread over the squares. Fold over the edges, and press firmly together after first brushing with egg white. Bake in medium-hot oven (400°F./Gas mark 6) for 35 minutes.

Ham Croissants *Schinkengipfeli*

1 lb. 2 oz. puff pastry or 'mock' puff paste (use equal parts flour, butter and cottage cheese)
8 oz. chopped cooked ham
1 egg
1 finely chopped onion
1 egg for brushing

Mix ham, egg and onion to a smooth, moist paste. Roll puff paste thinly and cut out small triangles. Place a spoonful of the filling on each triangle and roll it up, starting from the base. Curve it slightly, brush with egg yolk. The finished result will resemble a croissant. Rinse a baking sheet in cold water, place triangles on it and bake in a hot oven (425°F./Gas mark 7) for 12–15 minutes.

Cheese Tarts (see p. 18)

Apple Rolls *Apfelweggen*

Stealing or begging mother's best apple and taking it to the baker's before school is one of the memories of many a Swiss childhood. During break, it was fetched from the baker, nicely wrapped in dough and freshly baked, with a thin sprinkling of sugar on top. These dumplings or 'apples in dressing-gowns' are easily made at home with short or puff paste. Or try the Apple Rolls below.

8 oz. puff paste or short pastry
1 lb. apples
2 oz. sugar
1 level teaspoon cinnamon
1 oz. raisins
1 egg for brushing

Peel and core apples, cut in shreds and immediately sprinkle with sugar to prevent discoloration. Roll out the dough, cut in squares and place on each a spoonful of apples, raisins, sugar and cinnamon mixed. Fold over edges and firmly press them together. Brush with egg yolk and bake in medium-hot oven (400°F./Gas mark 6), for 15–20 minutes.

DESSERTS

Bilberries

In the old Swiss kitchen, tarts, cakes or pastry were the usual dessert and other sweet dishes were a rarity; though today, of course, in restaurants, as in private homes, chocolate cream, Charlotte Russe, fruit salad and Peach Melba are eaten just as they are everywhere—they are international. Traditional Swiss cooking offers a number of cold blancmanges known as 'Köpfli', made with vanilla, caramel, semolina and so on (sometimes from blancmange powders now). In country districts, whipped cream keeps its place of honour for all special occasions, but for everyday in the home fresh fruit and yoghurt, with or without flavouring, have largely replaced heavier desserts altogether. Here, then, are just one or two recipes, but all of them worth attention.

Meringue Rings *Vacherin*

In Switzerland, the term 'Vacherin' can indicate either one of two different sorts of cheese, or else this dessert which is common in the Emmenthal—where eating has been developed to a fine art. It is served at the end of an enormous meal of pork chops and fried potatoes, when it is hardly possible to eat any more.

little oil
little flour
6 egg whites
10 oz. icing sugar
1 pint cream
little vanilla-flavoured sugar

Line large baking sheet with greaseproof, oil it and sprinkle with flour. Whisk the egg whites, gradually adding half the sifted sugar. Lightly fold in rest of sifted sugar, fill mixture into a forcing pipe and squeeze three rings of equal size with a star-shaped pipe on to the baking sheet. It is advisable to trace the outlines first with a knife: the diameter of each should be about 5 inches. Before baking, sprinkle rings with vanilla sugar and allow to dry in very cool oven (240°F./Gas mark ¼)—leave oven door ajar—for about 1 hour.

The rings should now be only slightly tinged with gold and firm but not hard. Immediately place baking sheet on a damp cloth, carefully lift off rings, leave to cool. Spread little whipped, sweetened cream on a cake dish, place the first ring on it, spread with whipped cream, add the second ring and so on. Pour whipped cream over the top and decorate with cream, using the forcing pipe.

Vermicelles with Cream *Vermicelles mit Schlagrahm*

There are chestnut tarts, or simply the 'Vermicelles' themselves—chestnut purée piled in small pyramids and topped with cream—to be found in every pastrycook's in Switzerland.

Tins of chestnut purée are readily available and simplify the procedure at home. The following recipe uses fresh chestnuts and, of course, made this way the flavour is considerably better. So try it if you have the time, and substitute prepared purée otherwise.

2¼ lb. Spanish chestnuts
7½ fl. oz. milk
1 vanilla pod
little salt
2 oz. butter
3 oz. sugar

Make a cross-cut in the curved side of each chestnut and place on baking sheet in hot oven, or plunge into boiling water. After a few minutes cooking, the hard shell and brown skin beneath can easily be removed. Put chestnuts in saucepan, add water so that they are just covered, and boil for about 45 minutes. Add milk and vanilla pod, or a small piece of vanilla-flavoured sugar; cook and stir until liquid is absorbed. Pass through a sieve and add salt, sugar and butter while mixture is still hot. When cool, pass the mixture through a mincer to produce the characteristic 'wormlike' threads, and decorate small heaps with whirls of whipped cream.

Zabaione *Zabaione*
[Tessin]

This foamy dessert is a version of the Italian dish, also known under the name of 'Chaudeau' and served particularly in the Tessin, in wine glasses or coffee cups.

Per person:
1 egg yolk
1 tablespoon sugar
2 tablespoons white wine (or half wine, half water)

Mix all ingredients thoroughly. Place mixing bowl over pan of hot water and beat constantly with whisk until foamy. Do not allow to boil: remove mixture from heat just *before* it boils and pour into glasses or cups. Serve tepid.

Fruit and Milk Pudding *Heidelbeerbrei*
[Canton Bern]

Very popular with children. This recipe serves 8.

2¼ lb. bilberries (or other berries)
5½ oz. sugar
3¾ oz. white bread, cut in small cubes
2 oz. butter or fat
10 fl. oz. milk
sugar and ground cinnamon for topping

Wash and drain bilberries and mash in a bowl, together with the sugar. Fry the cubes of bread in butter until golden and add to the fruit, with the cold milk. Sprinkle with sugar and cinnamon, and serve.

Toggenburg Elderberry Purée *Toggenburger Holder-Mus*
[Canton St Gallen]

1½ oz. butter
1 tablespoon flour
1½ lb. elderberries (or other berries)
good ¼ pint milk
4 oz. sugar
sugar and cinnamon for topping

Fry flour in butter until light golden, pour in milk (or half cream, half milk), add the washed elderberries and the sugar and cook on low heat until the mixture is reduced to a thick purée, stirring constantly. Sprinkle with sugar and cinnamon, and serve.

A Well-brought-up Boy

A little boy from Landquart in the canton of Graubünden was on a visit to his godmother at Chur. After the main course, there followed a delicious tart which obviously pleased the young man very much indeed. When offered a second helping, he refused. Not even a small piece? No, thank you, quite sure. Five minutes later he burst into tears. His godmother anxiously asked what was the matter and he sobbed out the reply: 'At Landquart they *make* you have a second helping!'

OUT OF THE FRYING PAN

Muesli and Chuechli

Small cakes fried in lard, butter or oil used to play an important part in the kitchen. Almost every town in Switzerland had its own specialities with which to celebrate New Year or Carnival (the week before Ash Wednesday) or for everyday eating. There were 'rose cakes' and 'golden bonnets', 'knee rounds' (the dough was pulled as thin as possible on a cloth held over one knee), and many others with strange names. Then there were the many varieties of 'Strübli', and other regional specialities which must on no account be missed.

Sage Cakes *Salbeiküchlein*
[Zürich]

9 oz. plain flour
2 eggs
5 fl. oz. white wine
salt
sage leaves
fat
sugar

Mix together flour, salt, warmed wine and egg yolks to a smooth, thick batter. Leave to stand for 30 minutes. Immediately before frying, fold in beaten egg whites. Dip sage leaves in the batter and fry in deep fat until golden-brown. Sprinkle with sugar and pile on a dish.

Elderblossoms and mint leaves can be fried in the same way.

Fried Egg-Ball *Conterser Bock*

[Graubünden]

I have not been able to discover the significance of this strange name.

1 hard-boiled egg
pancake batter made with 3–4 eggs (see p. 72)
lard or butter for frying
sugar and ground cinnamon

Heat lard in sufficiently deep pan to give 3–4 inches of fat. Dip the shelled hard-boiled egg in the batter and fry in deep fat until golden. Lift out with a perforated spoon, again dip in batter and fry. Continue in this manner until all the batter has been used up and the egg-ball is quite large. Cut ball in quarters or eighths so that each segment contains part of the egg. Sprinkle with sugar and cinnamon, and serve with stewed apples. Alternatively, make a sauce with sweetened red wine, spiced with cinnamon, cloves and lemon rind, thicken with a little cornflour, and pour the sauce over the egg-ball.

Fried Spiced Cakes *Patlaunas*

[Engadine and Graubünden]

As the name indicates, these come from the Romansh-speaking area, which claims to have the most famous pastrycooks in the world.

10 oz. plain flour
2½ oz. butter
pinch of sodium bicarbonate
salt
2 small eggs
2½ fl. oz. cream
fat
sugar and ground cinnamon

Soften butter by heating slightly and work well into the flour; add salt and sodium bicarbonate. Stir together the cream and eggs and add mixture to the flour. Knead to a fairly firm dough and roll out thinly. Cut in lozenge-shaped pieces, making three slanting cuts in each. Fry in deep fat until lightly browned, and roll in sugar and cinnamon while still warm.

Egg Cakes *Eieröhrli*
[Zürich]

During the carnival period every Zürich bakery displays great heaps of these wavy, round cakes which are about the size of a pancake. There are many different recipes, some using milk or cream. The following is a genuine old Zürich recipe.

7 large or 8 small eggs
2 tablespoons melted butter
salt
1 lb. 2 oz. plain flour
fat
icing sugar

Beat the eggs for 15 minutes. Gradually add melted butter and little salt and after that, again gradually, the sifted flour. Form the soft dough into a roll and cut in pieces of about 2 oz. each. Cover with a cloth and leave for 30 minutes in a warm place. Roll out each piece of dough to a thin round cake and pull out further by hand—the thinner the better. If you want to pile these dough rounds one on top of the other, insert a paper napkin between them.

Heat plenty of fat in a saucepan, the bottom of which should be slightly smaller than the dough rounds. This gives them their waviness. Fry one round at a time. Use two wooden sticks or a wooden fork to keep them down, shape them and turn them. Drain the cakes on absorbent paper and while still warm, sprinkle with icing sugar. The cakes are at their best the day after they are made, but can be kept for 3–4 weeks.

Schenkeli *Schenkeli*

[Canton Bern]

4 oz. sugar
3 oz. butter
2 eggs
1 tablespoon Kirsch or rum
sugar and ground cinnamon
grated rind of 1 lemon
9 oz. plain flour
fat
pinch of salt

Beat butter and sugar until creamy and add eggs, Kirsch or rum, lemon rind and pinch of salt. Slowly add sifted flour and leave for 1 hour. Form dough into small finger-thick, finger-long rolls, just a little thicker at one end (hence the name 'shanks'). Fry in deep fat until lightly browned. If fat is not hot enough, the cakes absorb too much; if it is too hot, the cakes will have a bitter taste. They should split slightly down one side. Drain on absorbent paper, and sprinkle with sugar and cinnamon to taste. These cakes may be kept for a few days.

The dough may equally be formed by hand into almond-shaped pieces and fried as above. These are known as Bernese 'Mutzenmandeln'.

Cheese Doughnuts *Ziegerkrapfen*

For the dough:

9 oz. flour
5 fl. oz. milk
1½ oz. butter
pinch of salt

For the filling:

4 oz. cottage cheese
3 tablespoons cream
little ground cinnamon
1½ oz. raisins
2 oz. sugar
1 egg
2 oz. almonds

fat
sugar and ground cinnamon

Boil the milk with the butter and salt, add sifted flour and stir until mixture comes away easily from the bottom of the saucepan. Knead the dough on a board, roll out and cut round shapes with the rim of a cup. Pass cottage cheese through a sieve and mix with the other filling ingredients (add almonds blanched and grated). Stir until foamy. Place a spoonful of the filling in the centre of each circle of dough, moisten the edges with water or egg white and press firmly together so the cracks do not show. Fry doughnuts in deep fat on both sides and while still hot, sprinkle with sugar and cinnamon.

Funnel Cakes *Berner Strübli*

These are often known as 'funnel cakes', because the dough is poured through a funnel into the hot fat.

just under 1 pint milk
¾ oz. butter
12 oz. plain flour
pinch of salt
1 dessertspoon sugar
3 eggs
butter or lard for frying
sugar and ground cinnamon

Melt butter in warm milk (or instead of milk and butter, 2½ fl. oz. cream and ¾ pint hot white wine may be used). Stir together with the sifted flour, salt and sugar. Add the beaten eggs. If necessary, add another egg—the dough must be thin enough to run through a funnel.

Heat the fat. Hold funnel above saucepan of fat, pour in a ladleful of dough and move the funnel quickly spiralwise over the fat, in wider and wider circles from the central point so that a round cake is formed. Fry till light brown on both sides, and sprinkle with sugar and cinnamon while still hot.

If a savoury cake is preferred, omit the sugar and add little more salt to the dough, and finally sprinkle with salt and caraway seeds.

Fried Kranz Ring *Gebackener Kranz*

This is a popular dessert and its shape is a little out of the ordinary.

9 oz. tart apples (or other fruit)
sugar and cinnamon
1 small glass Kirsch

For the batter:

5½ oz. plain flour
2 egg yolks
10 fl. oz. beer or white wine
1 dessertspoon oil
1 dessertspoon Kirsch
fat for frying

Peel, core and finely chop the apples, sprinkle with sugar, cinnamon and Kirsch, and leave in a covered dish for 2 hours. Instead of apples, other fruit such as plums, cherries, or mixed fruit may be used. Prepare batter: sift flour into a bowl, blend in eggs, beer, oil and Kirsch, and leave for 2 hours.

To fry, use a straight-sided saucepan, not too large in diameter (about 6–7 inches). Pour in oil or fat to a depth of 1½–2 inches, heat. Mix fruit with the batter and pour batter, a little at a time, into the hot fat, pouring all round the saucepan, close to the sides. Add first one layer, then the next, until all the batter has been used. With a basting ladle, scoop fat from the middle and baste the ring, which should be moved occasionally with a fork to prevent it sticking to the sides of the saucepan. Turn ring carefully and fry on the other side until crisp and brown. Sprinkle with sugar and cinnamon and serve warm.

PASTRIES, CAKES AND BISCUITS

Swiss chocolate and the Engadine pastrycooks have joined forces to give Switzerland a reputation for fine baking throughout the world. The very high quality of pastries on sale has slightly damped some house-wives' enthusiasm for baking; but there remain many women who still prefer to bake their own cakes and tarts and, especially, Christmas fare, from the traditional recipes.

Engadine Nut Cake *Engadiner Nusstorte*
[Graubünden]

This resembles the Vienna Sachertorte in that the recipe is jealously guarded by pastrycooks and passed on from father to son.

12 oz. plain flour
9 oz. butter
7½ oz. sugar
2 eggs

For the filling:

10 oz. sugar
7½ oz. walnut kernels
5 fl. oz. cream
1 tablespoon honey
2 tablespoons red currant jelly

Quickly mix all ingredients, other than those for the filling, with cool hands (rinse them under the cold tap) to a dough. Leave to stand in a cool place for 20 minutes. Roll out two-thirds of the dough to approx. $\frac{1}{8}$-inch thickness and line bottom and sides of a 9-inch sandwich cake tin. Spread red currant jelly on the dough and leave to set a little before adding the filling.

For the filling, brown sugar slightly, without adding water, but do not let it get too dark. Add walnuts, which should also be fried for a moment or two. Pour in cream, add honey. Spread filling evenly over the dough. Form a lid from the remaining dough and cover the filling. Pierce lid in a few places with fork and bake in medium-hot oven (425°F./Gas mark 7) for 30 minutes. Do not use cake too soon; like all pastry containing honey, it should be kept for a few days.

Carrot Cake *Rüeblitorte*
[Canton Aargau]

9 oz. carrots, peeled and grated
10 oz. ground almonds
10 oz. sugar
5 eggs
2 oz. plain flour
1 teaspoon baking powder
grated rind of $\frac{1}{2}$ lemon
pinch of salt

For the icing:

5$\frac{1}{2}$ oz. icing sugar
1 tablespoon water
2 tablespoons lemon juice
small marzipan carrots for decoration
little jam

Beat together the egg yolks and sugar till foamy, add lemon rind, almonds, carrots, and sifted flour mixed with the baking powder and salt. Shortly before baking, fold in stiffly beaten egg whites and turn into a well-greased and floured cake tin. Bake in medium-hot oven (425°F./Gas mark 7) for 50 minutes. Leave to cool. Thoroughly mix sugar with lemon juice and water, and coat cold cake with this icing, after first brushing with thinned-down jam (preferably apricot). Decorate with marzipan carrots and keep till the following day, at the earliest, before serving.

Zug Cherry Cake *Zuger Kirschtorte*

Zug lies almost exactly midway between Zürich and Lucerne, and its pleasant countryside contains thousands and thousands of cherry trees—part of the harvest goes to the distilleries which produce the famous Zug Kirsch. This rose-coloured Cherry Cake, which all bakeries in Zug and the best in other parts of the country display, is not the ordinary kind of cherry cake (known as *Chriesitorte*) but a combination of two different kinds of pastry with butter cream and Kirsch, and equally popular with men!

The ingredients are sufficient for two medium-sized cakes, for it is hardly any more trouble to make two instead of one—and the second makes a highly acceptable present. This recipe is one for the experienced cook.

For the basic cake mixture:

5 egg whites
3¾ oz. ground almonds or hazelnuts (or half and half)
5½ oz. sugar
¾ oz. flour

For the biscuit layer:

5 eggs
5½ oz. sugar
7 oz. plain flour
grated rind of ½ lemon
3 oz. butter

For the butter cream:

9 oz. unsalted butter
4¾ oz. icing sugar
1 egg yolk
4 tablespoons Kirsch
red colouring

For assembling cake:

7½ oz. roasted almonds (half grated, half chopped)
10 fl. oz. Kirsch
2½ fl. oz. sugar water (water boiled with 2 tablespoons sugar)
icing sugar

1. Cake mixture: beat egg whites with half the sugar until stiff. Add almonds and sift in remaining ingredients and mix carefully. Divide mixture between four round well-greased cake tins of equal size. Bake in cool oven (310°F./Gas mark 2) until light brown (experts recommend leaving oven door ajar). for about 1 hour.

Remove rounds immediately from tins, if necessary holding over a saucepan of boiling water, and turn on to a flat dish to cool.

2. Biscuit layer: lightly whisk the eggs and sugar in a warm mixing bowl until thick and foamy, add lemon rind. Very lightly sift in the flour—if stirred too hard, the mixture collapses. Finally add the melted (but cooled) butter a trickle at a time, and mix lightly. Divide mixture between two greased baking tins, sprinkled with breadcrumbs (or lined with greaseproof), of the same diameter as those used for the cake rounds. Bake in preheated oven (400°F./Gas mark 6) for 30–45 minutes. Leave to cool, if necessary for some hours.

3. Butter cream: beat butter until white and creamy. Gradually add icing sugar and egg yolk. Tint mixture with a drop of red colouring. Add Kirsch at the last moment only, so that the aroma does not evaporate.

4. To assemble each cake: cut off the rounded top of the biscuit layer, leaving a flat circle approx. 1⅛ inches thick. Spread butter cream (with Kirsch added) on the first cake round. Generously lace biscuit layer with Kirsch and sugar water; place on top of cake round, pour over more Kirsch, then spread with butter cream. Place second cake round on top, and spread top and sides of the cake with butter cream. Sprinkle sides with chopped almonds, so that they stick to the cream. Sprinkle top with the grated almonds through a sieve and sift fairly thick layer of icing sugar over that. With the back of a knife, lightly trace diamond pattern on top of the cake. Leave in a cool place for several hours.

Chocolate Cherry Cake *Kirschentorte mit Schokolade*

[Canton Graubünden]

5 eggs
4¾ oz. castor sugar
4¾ oz. almonds, grated but not peeled
4¾ oz. grated plain chocolate
3¾ oz. breadcrumbs
3 dessertspoons Kirsch
grated rind of 1 lemon
10 oz. black cherries (tinned if necessary)

Thoroughly mix together 1 whole egg, 4 egg yolks and the sugar. Add grated almonds, chocolate, breadcrumbs, lemon rind and Kirsch. Finally fold in stiffly beaten egg whites, and turn into greased and floured cake tin. Carefully arrange the stalked fresh, or well-drained tinned cherries on top and bake in medium-hot oven (380°F./Gas mark 5) for about 1 hour.

Neuchâtel Flat Cake *Blechkuchen nach Neuenburger Art*

1 lb. 2 oz. rich shortcrust pastry
3¾ oz. castor sugar
2 oz. flour
1 wine glass white wine
1 teaspoon ground cinnamon
2 oz. butter

Roll out dough and place on baking sheet with rim. Prick with a fork. Mix together sugar and flour and sprinkle mixture over dough. Carefully pour over the wine with cinnamon added, but do not let it go over the edge. Dot with small pieces of butter and bake in a hot oven (425°F./Gas mark 7) for about 30 minutes, until golden-brown.

Waadtland Flat Cake *Blechkuchen nach Waadtländer Art*

1 lb. Yeast Dough (see p. 76)
approx. 10 fl. oz. cream
3 oz. sugar

Spread dough over baking sheet and leave for 10 minutes. Sprinkle with the sugar and pour over cream. Bake in medium-hot oven (400°F./Gas mark 6) for 30 minutes, till light brown in colour.

Glarn Jam and Almond Pastry *Glarner Pastete*
[Canton Glarus]

The double filling of almond paste and plum jam makes this a delicious example of the skill with sweet baking in eastern Switzerland.

1½ lb. puff paste (or 'mock' puff paste made from equal parts butter, flour and cottage cheese)
14 oz. plum jam
1 egg for brushing
icing sugar

For the almond paste:

4½ oz. ground almonds
3¾ oz. sugar
2 egg yolks
1¾ oz. butter
juice and rind of ½ lemon

For the almond paste, soften butter and beat with sugar and egg yolks until foamy. Add finely ground almonds, lemon juice and grated lemon rind. Divide dough into two, one part larger than the other. Roll out smaller part to approx. 2-inch thickness, cut a circle about 10–12 inches in diameter and place on a baking sheet rinsed in cold water. Spread plum jam on one half of the circle, and almond paste on the other, but leave a clear rim about 1½ inches all round and brush this with egg white. Roll out remaining dough to the same thickness as before and press over the jam/almond paste. Firmly press edges of dough together and trim off any overlap of the cover. Make regular indentations to form a scalloped edge. With scissors, cut the lid at intervals from the outer edge towards the centre. These cuts burst open in baking and allow a glimpse of the filling. Brush the top with egg yolk and decorate with small shapes made from remains of the dough. Bake for 40 minutes in hot oven (425°F./Gas mark 6). Do not open oven door during the first half of the baking time. Sprinkle with icing sugar while still warm.

Instead of one large pastry several small ones may be made.

Pear Bread *Birnbrot*

[Glarus]

2¾ lb. dried pears (or use fresh ones)
1 wine glass red wine (optional)
knob of butter (optional)
1 lb. 6 oz. grapes
4¾ oz. candied lemon peel
12 oz. walnut halves
2½ oz. ground cinnamon
½ oz. ground cloves
10 fl. oz. rosewater
2½ fl. oz. Kirsch
2¾ lb. bread dough

For the pastry:

2¾ lb. plain flour
1 lb. 10 oz. fat or butter
6 egg yolks
salt
milk or water
egg for brushing

Stalk and core dried pears and soak overnight (peel, core and slice fresh pears). Cook in some of the soaking water (for fresh pears, cook in scant ¼ pint water and 2 oz. sugar) and, if desired, with 1 glass red wine and knob of butter. When tender pour off remaining liquid. Pound or mash the pears and drain thoroughly; add other ingredients (except the dough) chopped finely. Leave overnight in a warm place. Knead together the mixture and the bread dough and form small loaves. Mix pastry dough and roll out not too thinly (1¾ lb. bread dough well mixed with 9 oz. butter may be used instead); divide into as many parts as there are loaves. Loosely wrap each small loaf in a piece of dough in such a way that the smooth surface is on top and the overlapping edges at the bottom. Prick the dough with a fork. Place loaves on greased, floured baking sheet, spacing them out well, and leave to rise. Brush with beaten egg and bake in a hot oven (400°F./Gas mark 6) for 1 hour. The loaves can be stored for a long time.

Pear Rolls *Birnwecken*

These are very similar to Pear Bread but smaller, and the filling consists of chopped fruit without being mixed with dough.

2¼ lb. dried pears (or fresh pears)
10 oz. prunes
4 oz. figs
9 oz. walnut halves
7½ oz. seedless raisins
4 oz. candied peel
5½ oz. sugar
¾ oz. cinnamon
¼ oz. powdered cloves
5 tablespoons Kirsch or lemon juice
2¼ lb. short pastry, yeast dough or puff paste
egg for brushing

Soak the dried fruit in water (or half water, half wine) for 1–2 days, cook for 20 minutes in the liquid in which they have soaked, and drain. Alternatively prepare and boil fresh pears for 5 minutes in ¼ pint water, drain well. Remove stones from the prunes, and chop with the pears. Coarsely chop figs and nuts, shred peel and wash raisins, and mix these with pears, prunes, sugar, spices and Kirsch or lemon juice.

Roll out dough to ⅛-inch thickness and cut in oblong pieces. Spread the filling ⅜-inch thick on each piece, leaving ¾-inch edge all round. Fold over the long sides, so that no filling can escape. Then roll up the dough and press edges together, brushing them with egg white if necessary. Arrange rolls, smooth side upwards, on floured baking sheet and brush with egg. Make scratches crosswise on the surface with a fork and prick here and there. Bake in medium oven (400°F./Gas mark 6) for 30–45 minutes (according to size), until light brown.

Polenta Cake *Polenta-Kuchen*

[Central Switzerland]

1¾ pints milk
4 eggs
3¾ oz. sugar
pinch of salt
1 oz. flour
12 oz. semolina
3¾ oz. butter
2¼ oz. raisins
3 apples
2½ fl. oz. cream
ground cinnamon

Mix together 2½ fl. oz. milk, 2 eggs, 2 oz. sugar, flour and pinch of salt, as for a pancake batter, and leave on one side. Stir semolina into rest of the milk, bring to the boil and add half the butter. Boil again, stirring frequently, until reduced to a thick porridge consistency. Leave to cool. Mix batter with the raisins and apples, peeled and cut in pieces, and with the semolina mixture. Turn into well-greased cake tin. Level the surface and make holes in it with the handle of a wooden spoon. Mix 2 remaining eggs with remaining sugar, cream and cinnamon, and pour over mixture in tin. Fill holes with flakes of butter and bake in a medium-hot oven (425°F./Gas mark 7) for 1 hour.

BISCUITS: GUETZLI AND ZELTLI

'Guetzli' are literally 'goodies' and both terms are used for biscuits or sweets. At Christmas, especially, they come into their own. Here are some favourite Swiss recipes.

Almond Biscuits *Brunsli mit Mandeln*

9 oz. grated unpeeled almonds
9 oz. castor sugar
2 egg whites
3½ oz. grated plain chocolate
pinch of cinnamon

Mix all ingredients, including the lightly whisked egg whites, with spoonful of water to a firm paste. Roll out on a sugared board to finger thickness. Cut out shapes—crescents, hearts, stars—and arrange, not too close together, on a buttered baking sheet. Bake in cool oven (335°F./Gas mark 3) for about 20 minutes. They must not become dry or hard.

Hazelnut Biscuits *Brunsli mit Haselnüssen*

9 oz. grated hazelnuts
9 oz. castor sugar
1½ tablespoons flour
2 tablespoons cocoa
1 egg white
1 dessertspoon water

Mix sugar and egg white and beat for a few minutes. Then add cocoa, hazelnuts, flour, and dessertspoon of cold water and proceed as for Almond Biscuits above. This recipe uses cocoa in place of chocolate, but the resulting biscuit has an equally nice flavour.

Aniseed Biscuits *Badener Kräbeli*
[Aargau]

These biscuits keep well for a long time.

1 lb. 2 oz. castor sugar
4 eggs
juice and rind of 1 lemon
2 tablespoons aniseed
1 lb. 2 oz. plain flour

Beat together sugar and eggs until foamy and able to hold their own shape. This may take quite a long time, though less if icing sugar is used. Add juice and rind of 1 lemon and the aniseed. Gradually sift in the flour (keeping back 2–3 spoonfuls for working the dough) until mixture has the consistency of a firm dough. Form dough into a long finger-thick roll and cut crosswise into pieces about ¾ oz. each. Flatten each piece slightly in the middle and curve into a horseshoe shape, making 3–4 slanting cuts on the top. Arrange on a buttered baking sheet and leave at average room temperature for at least 12 hours. On the following day, bake in cool oven (335°F./Gas mark 3) for about 20 minutes. They should be pale yellow in colour.

Milanese Biscuits *Mailänderli*

No one knows why these crisp golden stars, hearts and crescents are called 'Milanese', but in Switzerland they are the most popular of all for Christmas.

1 lb. 2 oz. plain flour
9 oz. sugar
9 oz. butter
3 eggs
grated rind of 1 lemon
salt
1 egg yolk for brushing

Cut butter in small pieces and mix all ingredients (except egg yolk) quickly and thoroughly. Quickly knead together, with cool hands, and leave paste for 30 minutes or longer in a cold place. Roll out to ⅛-inch thickness, cut out stars, hearts and crescents and arrange on buttered baking sheet. Brush with egg yolk and bake in a medium-hot oven (400°F./Gas mark 6) for 20 minutes or until golden.

Spagnoletti *Spagnoletti*
[Canton Graubünden]

9 oz. castor sugar
3 egg yolks
3 whole eggs
grated rind of ½ lemon
9 oz. plain flour
9 oz. peeled, finely chopped almonds

Beat sugar with egg yolks and the grated lemon rind until creamy; then add the whole eggs, one at a time. Fold in the sifted flour. Grease and flour baking sheet and with a spoon, arrange small piles of mixture on the sheet. Sprinkle lightly with chopped almonds. Tilt baking sheet slightly to remove loose bits of almond. Bake in a very cool oven (310°F./Gas mark 2) for about 30–40 minutes, until just lightly golden.

Dead Men's Bones *Totenbeinli*

A somewhat macabre name—and in a tin with a well-fitting lid, these 'bones' keep for a long time!

3 oz. butter
9 oz. castor sugar
3 eggs
salt
9 oz. blanched, chopped almonds
½ tablespoon ground cinnamon
12 oz. plain flour
1 egg yolk for brushing

Soften butter, add sugar and beat until white and creamy. Add one egg at a time, then the almonds, cinnamon, salt and finally the sifted flour. Knead paste well and shape into an oblong about 1½ inches thick. Leave in a cold place until quite firm. Cut paste into 2½–3-inch-long fingers and brush with egg yolk. Bake in medium-hot oven (400°F./Gas mark 6) for 20 minutes until just golden.

Cinnamon Biscuits *Zimt-Pitte*
[Graubünden]

Graubünden is a Romansh-speaking district and many terms are borrowed from the Italian, such as, for instance, the word 'Pitte' from the Italian *pizza. Zimt-Pitte* are a cinnamon-flavoured shortbread. The following recipe comes from Chur.

For the paste:

1½ oz. sugar
14 oz. grated unpeeled almonds
9 oz. butter
10 oz. plain flour
2 oz. ground cinnamon
3 egg yolks
1 whole egg

For the topping:

4¾ oz. peeled almonds, cut in strips
4¾ oz. castor sugar
3 egg whites

Quickly and thoroughly knead together the ingredients for the paste; roll out not too thinly and place over buttered and well-floured baking sheet. Beat 3 egg whites, mix with sugar and almonds, and spread over paste. Cut into diamond-shaped pieces and bake in medium oven (400°F./Gas mark 6) for 20 minutes, until lightly browned. Lift off sheet while still warm.

Dripping Biscuits *Feula-Pitte*

In Switzerland, the remains left when dripping is made are called by various names, one of them 'Feula'. Hence the name of the following recipe, which comes from the Upper Engadine.

3¾ oz. dripping
4–5 tablespoons milk
2 egg yolks
6¾ oz. castor sugar
4¾ oz. raisins
2½ oz. grated almonds
1 teaspoon ground cinnamon
12 oz. plain flour

Slightly warm dripping with the milk and stir together. Mix with other ingredients, gradually adding the flour last of all (10 oz. flour may be sufficient). When paste has the consistency of a soft cake-mixture, spread on well-buttered and floured baking sheet and with a pointed knife cut into lozenge-shaped pieces. Bake in medium-hot oven (400°F./Gas mark 6) for 15–20 minutes until light brown and break along the lines.

Spicy Sugar Rusks *Triätschnitten*

These red, spicy, sugary biscuits are gradually being forgotten, but some bakers still make them and certainly some of the older housewives, who like to keep them in store as an invaluable standby.

1 tablespoon cochineal (or other red colouring)
¾ oz. ground cinnamon
½ oz. nutmeg
¼ oz aniseed
¼ oz. powdered cloves
icing sugar
stale bread, at least 2 days old
10 oz. sugar
10 fl. oz. water

Mix colouring with cinnamon, nutmeg, aniseed and cloves; and with each 1 level teaspoon of this powder mix 3¾ oz. icing sugar. Slice bread (to rusk thickness). Boil sugar and water till it 'blows' (when a wire loop is dipped in the solution it should be covered with a thin film that can be blown off). First dip one side of each slice of bread in the sugar syrup, sprinkle with the red spice powder and leave to dry on a baking sheet in a warm—not hot—oven (355°F./Gas mark 4) for 20 minutes. Then dip slices on the other side and proceed in the same way. Finally sprinkle the warm, dry rusks again with the powder and leave to cool. They keep very well.

Macaroons *Amaretti*

Anyone who likes the taste of bitter almonds will prefer these macaroons to all other biscuits.

- 7½ oz. sweet and 3¾ oz. bitter almonds
- 1 lb. 2 oz. castor sugar
- 2 egg whites
- icing sugar

Peel almonds and leave to dry for at least a day, then grind. Mix almonds with egg whites, sift in castor sugar and knead together thoroughly. Line baking sheet with paper and arrange on it walnut-sized heaps of the mixture, spacing them out well. Dry rather than bake in oven (335°F./Gas mark 3) for about 30 minutes. Dust with icing sugar while still warm. If they stick to the paper, moisten it with cold water.

Honey Biscuits *Basler Leckerli*

The Swiss Cook, a Modern Bernese Cookery Book for Town and Country, published in 1870, contains no less than eight different recipes for 'Basler Leckerli', among them two 'minor varieties'! These 'very fine' biscuits are still equal to any modern recipe.

- approx. 2¼ lb. honey
- 1 lb. 2 oz. sugar
- 1 lb. 2 oz. peeled, sliced almonds
- pinch of nutmeg
- chopped rind of 2 thinly peeled lemons
- 2¾ lb. plain flour (put in warm place on day before use)
- 6 oz. chopped candied lemon and orange peel
- 2 oz. ground cinnamon
- ½ oz. powdered cloves
- 1 teaspoon baking powder (optional)
- 1 glass Kirsch

For the icing:

1 lb. 2 oz. icing sugar and 1 pint water, boiled until threads can be pulled out when a little of the syrup is tested between 2 spoons

Bring honey to the boil, add sugar and again bring to the boil. Add almonds, chopped peel, cinnamon, cloves, nutmeg, lemon rind, stirring constantly. Remove from heat and gradually sift in flour and baking powder if used. Pour over Kirsch and light. Blow out flames immediately and mix paste thoroughly with a wooden spatula. Leave in warm place for about 1 hour; then knead by hand. Dust a board with flour, place on it a portion of the paste at a time, knead again and then roll out to about ¼-inch thickness. Cut into oblongs about 1½ × 2 inches. Place close together on buttered, well-floured baking sheet and leave overnight or even for two or three days. Bake in medium-hot oven (400°F./Gas mark 6) for about 30 minutes. Cut apart on baking sheet while still hot and brush with sugar icing (see above) which should immediately dry and turn white.

In a tin with well-fitting lid, these biscuits keep for a long time.

In the original recipe no mention is made of any raising agent and if pure honey is used none may be necessary. But 1 teaspoon baking powder may be added.

Zürich Marzipan Biscuits *Zürcher Marzipanleckerli*

Apart from 'Basler Leckerli', there are Leckerli from Bern and St Gallen and Zürich, and other varieties which all, however, bear a close resemblance and are only really different in the proportions of honey, sugar and flour used. But these Marzipan Leckerli from Zürich are quite separate.

1 lb. 2 oz. ground almonds
1 oz. ground bitter almonds
1 lb. 2 oz. icing sugar
2 eggs
approx. 2 tablespoons rosewater or orange-blossom water

For the icing:

9 oz. icing sugar
1 egg white
2 tablespoons orange-blossom water or lemon juice

Mix ground almonds with sifted icing sugar, add egg whites and 2 tablespoons rosewater and place mixing bowl in a saucepan of water over heat. Beat until the mixture begins to come away easily from the bottom of the bowl. Remove bowl and add lightly beaten egg yolks. Dust board with icing sugar and roll out the paste to approx. ⅜-inch thickness. Cut out oblongs about 1½ × 2 inches and place on board dusted with flour; brush with more rosewater and leave for 2 days at average room temperature. Butter a baking sheet, dust with flour and dry rather than bake the Leckerli for 15 minutes in cool oven (310°F./Gas mark 2). Mix icing ingredients till smooth. After baking, immediately brush biscuits with the icing. If a large number are made at one time, they look most attractive if a mixture of colours and flavours are used for the icing, for instance, chocolate, lemon and raspberry. Alternatively, the basic marzipan paste itself may be divided before it is rolled out and coloured and flavoured with chocolate and pistachio respectively.

Nut and Honey Biscuits *Honigleckerli*

This recipe uses no flour.

4 oz. ground hazelnuts
4 oz. ground unpeeled almonds
2 egg whites
2 oz. chopped candied peel
9 oz. castor sugar
2 tablespoons honey
4 tablespoons icing sugar
½ egg white or little lemon juice for icing

Mix almonds, hazelnuts, sugar, honey, candied peel and 2 egg whites and knead into rollable mixture. Leave in a cool place for 30 minutes or longer. Thickly dust board with icing sugar, place paste on it and roll out to approx. ¼-inch thickness. Cut into diamond-shaped pieces and arrange, not too close together, on a buttered, floured baking sheet. Bake in cool oven (335°F./Gas mark 3) for 20–30 minutes. While still warm coat with the mixed icing sugar, egg white and lemon juice. Leave for some days before eating.

Biberli *Biberli*

[St Gallen]

Popular Christmas fare. There is a plain and a stuffed variety.

12 oz. honey
7 oz. sugar
1 teaspoon ground cinnamon
½ teaspoon powdered cloves
pinch of grated nutmeg
1 lb. 5 oz. plain flour
2 tablespoons rosewater
¼ oz. potash
honey for brushing

For the stuffing:

4½ oz. peeled and grated almonds
4½ oz. sugar
2 tablespoons honey
2 tablespoons lemon juice or rosewater
1 egg white for brushing

Bring honey to the boil, add sugar, then the spices and gradually the flour, and the potash dissolved in rosewater. When dough is no longer sticky, roll out to approx. $\frac{1}{16}$-inch thickness, cut into small oblongs and leave overnight on a floured board. Next day, bake in medium-hot oven (400°F./Gas mark 6) for 20 minutes on greased or waxed baking sheet and while still warm, brush with melted honey. To make stuffed Biberli, mix finely ground almonds with sugar and lemon juice to a marzipan-like paste. Place 1 teaspoonful of the mixture on each dough oblong, brush the edges with egg white and fold over to form triangles. Leave overnight; bake the next day as above and brush with melted honey.

Cinnamon Honey Rings *Willisauer Ringli*

2 egg whites
9 oz. sugar
pinch of cinnamon
8 oz. plain flour
1 tablespoon honey

Whisk egg whites and gradually fold in sugar, sift in flour and cinnamon, and knead to a smooth paste. Leave in a cool place for 1 hour. Roll out to approx. ½-inch thickness and cut out rings with cutters or the rims of two glasses of different sizes. Bake in medium-hot oven (400°F./Gas mark 6) for 15 minutes until lightly browned and brush with melted honey while still hot.

Cream Bonbons *Nidelzeltli*

Not biscuits—but these sweets are great fun to make at a children's party particularly—and to eat!

- 1¾ pints liquid (half milk, half cream), or 1¾ pints milk and 2 teaspoons butter, or 1 pint milk and 1 tin sweetened condensed milk
- 1 lb. 2 oz. sugar

Bring sugar, milk and cream to the boil in not too small a saucepan (or it will boil over) and by constantly stirring, reduce to a thick yellowy-brown mixture which should come away easily from the bottom of the saucepan. Pour mixture on to a buttered edged baking sheet, spread to approx. ⅜-inch thickness and leave to cool for 10 minutes. Take a pointed knife, dip in oil and cut mixture in small squares. Allow to get cold, when the children can enjoy breaking up the finished sweets.

A NOTE ON DRINKS

Generally speaking, white wine is the most usual drink in western Switzerland, red wine in the Tessin, and white coffee throughout the rest of the country. This is not to say that coffee is not drunk in Geneva and Lugano, or wine in Zürich and Basle; but in German-speaking Switzerland, white coffee plays a special part, in the cities as well as in the country. It is the most common breakfast drink: equal parts of coffee and hot milk, generally without sugar, into which bread is crumbled. In restaurants it is served as 'Schale Gold' and 'Schale Hell'; and as '*Kaffee complet*' it comes with bread, butter, jam, and sometimes a piece of cheese, for lunch or supper. Light evening meals of fried potatoes, fritters, or Bircher Muesli, are all eaten with coffee, though non-Swiss find this less to their taste.

Wine is taken for granted as a daily drink in western and southern Switzerland and much wine is also consumed in other parts of the country. The white wines from Lakes Waadtland, Neuchâtel and Biel, white and red wines from Wallis and the *vin rosé* from eastern Switzerland, provide a wide choice. When 'Sauser', the young unfermented wine, is served during the grape harvest, a wave of high spirits runs through the whole country.

Of the distilled drinks, the Kirsch from Zug and Baselbiet is probably the best known. Specialities which cannot be found anywhere else are the Alpine herb schnaps of Appenzell, the apricot schnaps of Wallis and, in recent years, the 'Williamine' pear schnaps which is esteemed for its fruity aroma.

In the last few decades, sweet cider has become popular. Apple cider, pear cider and non-alcoholic white and red grape juice are excellent drinks with a meal and have become indispensible in most homes.

A FEAST FROM THE GOOD OLD DAYS . . .

This is a short diversion to round off the many traditional recipes in preceding chapters with an account of a traditional celebration. It is taken from Jeremias Gotthelf's *The Black Spider* and gives a splendid idea of the procedure.

'A christening was to be held at the house, and the midwife, who cooked as skilfully as she brought babies into the world would have to bustle if everything was to be ready on time and all the dishes which custom demands were to be prepared on the simple cooking range.

'A stocky man emerged from the cellar with a great piece of cheese in his hand. He took the nearest plate from the polished dresser, placed the cheese on it and made to carry it into the room and put it on the brown walnut-wood table. "But, Benz, Benz," cried the pale, handsome woman, "how they would mock if we had no finer plate for the christening." So she went to the shining cherrywood dresser . . . where the most valuable ornaments of the house were kept behind glass doors. She took a beautiful plate with a blue rim and a bouquet of flowers in the centre, surrounded by such rhymes as "It's hot in hell, the potter works well" and "The cow in grass doth lie, and man must surely die". Beside the cheese she placed the great twist of bread, the special Bernese bread, braided like the tresses of a woman, baked brown and yellow and made from the finest flour, eggs and butter—as big as a yearling child and almost as heavy. At either end she put two more plates, piled high with tempting cakes of one sort and another. Hot, thick cream in a flowery dish stood covered on the stove and the coffee boiled in a three-legged shining jug with a yellow lid. Then there was awaiting the godparents and guests a breakfast such as kings enjoy rarely and no peasants in the world except the Bernese. Thousands of Englishmen hasten through Switzerland, but none of the weary lords and stiff-legged ladies ever see such a breakfast.

'The midwife politely placed the godmother behind the table and the young wife came with the coffee. . . . Outside the two godfathers, one old, one young, refusing the new-fangled coffee which they could have every day, sat over the steaming old-fashioned Bernese wine soup, made with wine, toast, eggs, and cinnamon and saffron, the traditional spices which at a christening must be added to everything from soup to sweet tea.

The Christening Feast

'When finally all were seated round the table, there came the soup, a beautiful beef soup, coloured and spiced with saffron, and so thickly covered with the delicious white bread which the grandmother had cut into it that hardly anything of the liquid was to be seen. They all took off their hats, folded their hands and silently thanked the giver of all good things. Then only they took hold of the tin spoons, wiped them on the fine tablecloth and started on the soup. If they had soup like that every day, they said, they would wish for nothing better. When the soup was finished, the spoons were wiped again and the twists of bread handed round. Everyone cut his own piece and watched the serving of the entrée—brain, mutton and liver—in saffron gravy. When that had slowly disappeared, there came dishes piled high with beef, fresh and dried, to suit everyone's taste, with dried beans, dried pears, bacon and pork—wonderful joints from the backs of pigs which weighed at least three hundredweight, all pink and white, and juicy. Thus one course followed another, and when a new guest came he had to start from the beginning with the soup, and no one was allowed to forgo a single dish. Meanwhile Benz, the baby's father, kept filling the glasses from magnificent white quart bottles, richly decorated with crests and rhymes.

'Thus amid joking and laughter much meat was eaten and the dried pears were by no means neglected, until the older godfather finally thought that for the moment everyone had had their fill and would be all the better for stretching their legs. A pipe, he said, never tasted better than after meat. His advice was accepted with acclamation, in spite of the protests of the young parents. They thought that once the guests had left the table, they would not easily find their way back to it. "Don't worry," said the cousin. "If you put something else nice on the table you will have us back in no time and if we stretch a little now, we shall do all the more justice to your food afterwards." '

ORIGINAL Dr.Bircher

THE MODERN SWISS KITCHEN

To many people the 'Swiss kitchen' is a synonym for health-giving food and modern nutrition—for Bircher Muesli, raw carrots, wholemeal bread and brown sugar.

Efforts to evolve a diet conforming more closely to nature began in Switzerland a few decades earlier than anywhere else and were more widely accepted. The emergence of a new national dish, Bircher Muesli, is proof of the popularity of the food-reform movement, which had its starting-point and centre at Dr Bircher-Benner's private clinic in Zürich, founded in 1897. In 1907, Alice Bircher, Dr Bircher-Benner's sister, who managed the clinic, produced its first cookery book, which ran to several editions. By the time Ruth Kunz-Bircher, a daughter of Dr Bircher-Benner, published an enlarged *Bircher-Benner Cookery Book* in 1952, 'modern' nutritional methods and reform foods had become fashionable. In America, Gaylord Hauser began to advertise with every means of modern psychology a diet closely related to that which Dr Bircher-Benner had recommended half a century before.

The number of people who consciously and consistently advocated the Bircher diet was never particularly large, but their influence on the eating habits of the Swiss cannot be overestimated. Today there is hardly a family in Switzerland—and particularly in the German-speaking part—which does not consciously or unconsciously accept and practise some of the new principles. One of these is never to start a meal without some uncooked food (salad, fruit or vegetable juice, raw fruit). Great care is taken not to overcook vegetables, so as to preserve the vitamins, and to limit the intake of proteins; to eat less-refined foodstuffs, with nuts and dried fruit as snacks between meals, and to preserve the right balance between foods rich in acids and those rich in alkalis.

The woman who has done more than anyone else—with the exception of the Bircher family—to spread and popularize these principles is known to most people simply by her first name, Nelly. Frau Nelly Hartmann is editor of the only Swiss cookery journal, the monthly *Nelly's Calendar*. Recipes and menus printed in the journal have since 1948 translated the theories of modern nutrition into the everyday language of the housewife. They are arranged according to the seasons and are good for both vegetarians and meat-eaters.

Of course the food reformers did not invent raw food—Adam was taking 'raw food' when he bit the apple Eve gave him! But we know today that uncooked foods provide essential vitamins and mineral salts. Swiss women are particularly inventive in varying the possibilities of salads, fruit and vegetable juices, and so on, of which the following recipes give a few examples.

FRUIT AND VEGETABLE JUICES

If you possess a liquidizer attachment to your electric mixer, the extraction of fruit and vegetable juices presents no problem. Otherwise squeeze citrus fruits (oranges, lemons, grapefruit) in the ordinary way; shred apples, carrots, horseradish, cucumber, or celery, and press through a sieve. Tomatoes can be sliced and passed through a liquidizer, as can berries and grapes.

Apple Juice *Apfelsaft*

Wash apples and cut them, but do not peel or core. Liquidize and drink immediately. Lemon juice, cucumber juice, celery juice or carrot juice may be added.

Tomato Juice *Tomatensaft*

Mix freshly extracted tomato juice with 1 teaspoon lemon juice. Alternatively, add 2 dessertspoons orange juice and 2 dessertspoons cream to small glass of tomato juice.

Berry Juice *Beerensaft*

Pass any variety of berries through a strainer and drink with no other additions. A mixture of raspberry and red currant juice is particularly pleasant.

Sauerkraut Juice *Sauerkrautsaft*

Sauerkraut juice is an old cure for an upset stomach, but too much should not be taken. For a change, mix sauerkraut juice with little orange or apple juice, which makes it less tart.

SALADS

Traditional Mixed Salad *Salat von verschiedenen Kraütern*

'Take equal parts of celery, raw cabbage, endives, watercress, wash, and arrange separately in a bowl. Garnish with pickled beetroot and hard-boiled eggs, chopping whites and yolks separately.'

Taken from the *Swiss Cookery Book* by E. Landolt, 1842, this countermands any claim by food reformers to have invented the salad!

Salad Dressings *Die Salatsaucen*

I feel tempted to say that these depend on your philosophy! In the average Swiss kitchen, a thick dressing is made from vinegar, oil, salt, pepper, spices and, usually, chopped onions. Connoisseurs rub the inside of the salad bowl with garlic and swear by the classic recipe for wine vinegar, olive oil, salt and pepper, as the saying goes: Take vinegar like a miser, oil like a spendthrift, season like a sage and mix like a madman. Food reformers recommend a variety of salad dressings with oil, cream, yoghurt, cottage cheese, and almonds, but no vinegar, which is usually replaced by lemon juice, and with many chopped kitchen herbs for seasoning.

Spinach Salad *Spinatsalat*

Wash tender young spinach very thoroughly and immediately before the meal, toss in dressing of a spoonful of cream and a finely chopped onion.

Lettuce-Leaf Salad *Schnittsalat*

Mix young lettuce leaves (not the hearts) immediately before the meal with parsley, chopped basil or dill.

Cos Lettuce Salad *Lattichsalat*

The innermost, light-green leaves of the narrow cos heads are a delicacy. Leave them whole and dip into herb-flavoured mayonnaise. Bigger leaves may be cut in strips and served as a salad with a thinned mayonnaise.

Chicory Salad *Chicoreesalat*

Chicory heads may be shredded, which brings out the bitter taste, or the leaves separated, or heads halved or quartered. Serve with a dressing of red wine vinegar and olive oil; or with mayonnaise diluted with orange juice, sprinkling the chicory with chopped orange peel and walnuts.

Endive Salad *Grüner Chicoree*

When cleaning the endive, retain a piece of the root, scrape off the skin and divide the green heads into halves or quarters so that each has a little bit of root attached. Serve with a simple salad dressing.

Fennel Salad *Fenchelsalat*

Remove the tough outer leaves and the stalks. Shred fennel finely. Mix with lemon juice only, or a salad dressing, and sprinkle with chives and the chopped light-green fennel leaves.

Radish and Horseradish Salad *Radieschen- und Rettichsalat*

Horseradish and large 'overgrown' radishes go well together. Peel horseradish and wash radishes. Shred both on a vegetable grater. Serve with any dressing desired, sprinkle with chives and leave for 15 minutes before serving.

Celery Salad *Roher Sellerie als Salat*

Celery discolours easily. Slice the scraped celery and cut in thin slivers, or shred, and immediately mix with a thinned mayonnaise.

Kohlrabi Salad *Kohlrabi als Rohsalat*

Peel tender kohlrabis and shred on vegetable grater. Season the dressing with mustard and paprika, or a mixture of kitchen herbs.

Leek Salad *Lauchsalat*

Boiled leeks with a salad dressing make a popular hors d'oeuvre, as in France, Leeks may also be used raw as a salad: wash thoroughly and cut in thin slices. Serve with a mild, creamy mayonnaise and sprinkle with parsley.

Beetroot Salad *Randen als Rohsalat*

Beetroot salad is usually made with boiled beetroots, or beetroots baked in their skins in the oven; but they are almost tastier raw. Wash and clean the beetroots, peel, and shred straight into a salad dressing. Flavour with caraway seeds, chives or chopped onions.

Sauerkraut Salad *Sauerkrautsalat*

Uncooked sauerkraut is a favourite on food reformers' menus (they recommend the use of sauerkraut made from unmanured cabbage or, if that is impossible, washing the sauerkraut in a sieve under the tap). Use a rather mild dressing. Grate in a whole apple and mix with chopped herbs.

Mixed Salads *Mischsalate*

A gourmet's palate and an artist's eye are needed for the mixing of salads. Prepare sufficient dressing and only at the last moment mix with the well-drained ingredients, such as lettuce, chicory, young spinach, cress, tomatoes and, if liked, rings of red and green peppers. Sprinkle chopped walnuts over the finished salad. Alternatively, mix grated celery, diced apples, chicory, cos lettuce, and serve with horseradish-flavoured mayonnaise. Garnish with radishes and hard-boiled egg.

PRESENTING RAW VEGETABLES

An hors d'oeuvre of raw vegetables to start the meal is splendid for health. The vegetable platter should consist of three types: salad or green vegetables, a root vegetable, and a 'fruit' vegetable. Use greenstuff such as lettuce, cress, chicory and endive, cabbage, etc.; and mix with celery, carrots, horseradish, radish, kohlrabi or beetroot and, of the 'fruity' variety, tomatoes, cucumber, baby marrows, peppers. When preparing a large vegetable platter for a special occasion, remember not only to include some of each of the three groups, but also to pay attention to the colours, for raw vegetables in particular are savoured, in the first instance, by the eye.

Stuffed Tomatoes *Gefüllte Tomaten*

Mix cottage cheese with herbs, diced flesh of the tomatoes and little milk, and fill mixture into the tomato shells. Alternatively, mix shredded celery and diced apple with mayonnaise, and top with halved walnuts; or use raw, sliced mushrooms in mayonnaise dressing.

Cauliflower with Mayonnaise *Blumenkohl mit Mayonnaise*

Very good as a 'dip' at a cocktail party. Place cauliflower in salt water for about 1 hour to draw out and kill any slugs or worms. Detach flowerets, each with a small stalk, and spike with wooden toothpicks. Scoop out a red cabbage (use inside for salad) and fill with thick mayonnaise. Stick toothpicks into the cabbage, all round, so that it looks like a hedgehog. The guests remove the flowerets with the toothpicks and dip them in the mayonnaise.

Open Sandwiches *Rohkost-Sandwiches*

Next time you entertain, try making a large board of sandwiches, half with sausage, ham, hard-boiled egg, anchovy, etc., and the other half with cucumber, tomatoes, grated celery, cottage cheese mixed with herbs, and other vegetables. You may be surprised to find which half disappears first.

1. Butter slices of wholemeal bread and cover with shredded celery mixed with lemon juice (to prevent discoloration) and mayonnaise.
2. Cover wholewheat bread in the same way with grated carrots mixed with lemon juice.
3. Butter slice of rye bread, cover with lettuce leaf and top with cottage cheese and slices of radish.
4. Butter slices of oatmeal bread and cover with sliced cucumber or tomatoes. Sprinkle cucumber with chopped dill and tomatoes with chopped basil or chives.
5. Mix cottage cheese with salt and chopped chives. Spread on slices of crisp rye bread, arrange walnuts on top.
6. Thickly butter slices of toast and sprinkle with fresh cress.
7. Mix cottage cheese with cream and grated horseradish and spread on pumpernickel. Cottage cheese may also be seasoned with paprika and finely chopped onion.
8. Arrange lettuce leaves on slices of white bread, add tender lettuce leaves cut in strips and chopped tomatoes, and garnish with small slices of lemon or orange.

SWISS MUESLI

When the Bircher-Benner clinic was founded in Zürich in 1897, 'Bircher Muesli' did not appear on the menu—it was then called 'fruit diet'; but this dish was served so frequently that patients soon came to call it just 'the dish'. *The Bircher-Benner Cookery Book* (published by Bircher-Benner, Zürich-Frankfurt a.M.) has this to say:

'With Bircher Muesli, as it became known to the public, Dr Bircher-Benner basically reintroduced an old custom, for in the fruit-growing parts of Switzerland people used to be content with an evening meal of fruit, porridge, milk and, frequently, nuts. The fruit consisted of apples, pears, berries or dried fruit, according to season, the porridge of spelt (German wheat), oats or barley, and the milk was usually fresh and unboiled. Fruit—cereals—milk, the components of Muesli, form a time-honoured and very natural triad of dietetics, the nuts adding a special note to the harmony. In the old days, the various components were chopped up by strong teeth and mixed together in the stomach, instead of in the kitchen. The Bircher Muesli became so popular that Dr Bircher-Benner's patients introduced it into their homes. Friends and acquaintances asked for the recipe and many people came to know it long before its preparation was described in detail in the little book, *Fruit Dishes and Raw Vegetables*, published in 1924 by "Turning-Point". Many restaurants in Switzerland introduced Muesli. In Lausanne and Geneva the customer orders "*un Birche*" and often has no idea of the origin of the dish. Muesli may appear unexpectedly on the table in a lonely cowherd's cabin in the high Alps, as well as in a planter's house in the tropics. According to newspaper reports, Henry Ford became a Muesli convert, and a professor in Milan offered it to his guests as "*Dolce Sorpresa*". In England it is simply called "Swiss Muesli". It has become something of a national dish.'

Original Muesli *Birchermüesli*

Per person:

1 level tablespoon oatmeal
3 tablespoons cold water
1 tablespoon lemon juice
1 tablespoon sweetened tinned milk
8 oz. apples
1 tablespoon grated hazelnuts or almonds

Soak the oats in water for 12 hours (if quick-cooking oats are used, simply mix with water). Add lemon juice and tinned milk and grate unpeeled apples straight into the mixture. If necessary, add 1–2 tablespoons water. Sprinkle with grated nuts or almonds.

The above is the original Muesli, which can be varied according to taste and season. Use mashed strawberries or other berries, or thinly sliced apricots, plums or peaches, in place of apples. Combine several kinds of fruit, for instance, apples and bananas, apples and oranges, raspberries and red currants, blackberries and apples. Substitute 3 tablespoons yoghurt and 1 tablespoon honey for the tinned milk; or use wheat, millet, mixed cereal grains or soya in place of oats.

Muesli is not a dessert and should be eaten at the beginning of a meal. Its full value is not felt unless the appetite is keen and the stomach empty. It is particularly good for breakfast, or as an 'hors d'oeuvre' before an evening meal, with wholemeal bread and butter.

FRUIT DISHES

There is nothing more delicious than berries and cream, or whipped cream. Strawberries, wild strawberries, currants, bilberries—each is better than the next and at any time of the year, some fruit is available.

Yoghurt and Fruit *Yoghurt-Fruchtspeise*

Mix ⅓ pint yoghurt with juice of 1 orange, juice of ½ lemon, 1 grated apple, 1 chopped apple, 1 chopped pear, 1 mashed banana. Garnish with slices of banana and orange.

Strawberries and Oranges *Erdbeeren mit Orangen*

Wash and drain strawberries and arrange on a bed of thin-sliced oranges. Pour over orange juice and sprinkle with sugar.

Apple Purée *Creme aus rohen Äpfeln*

Grate 1 lb. 2 oz. apples and mix with juice of small grapefruit. Sweeten with brown sugar or honey and whisk until creamy. Fold in $\frac{1}{3}$ pint whipped cream and serve immediately.

Peach Cream *Rohe Pfirsichcreme*

Peel and dice 1 lb. 2 oz. peaches. Sweeten to taste and leave in covered dish. Whisk together $\frac{1}{3}$ pint yoghurt, $2\frac{1}{2}$ fl. oz. cream, 3 tablespoons sugar and 2 oz. grated almonds, or hazelnuts, until creamy, add peaches and leave in a cool place until ready to serve.

Cereals and Fruit *Flockenspeisen*

Almost any fruit is suitable for mixing with uncooked cereals: for instance, plums, cherry plums, greengages, cherries, or apricots. Wash fruit and cut in pieces, add sugar and leave for 30 minutes. Then mix with cereal and sprinkle with chopped nuts.

Orange and Banana Cream *Orangencreme mit Bananenrahm*

Mix 10 fl. oz. water with 3 oz. sugar and $\frac{1}{2}$ oz. powdered agar-agar or gelatine. Turn into fireproof dish and stir over medium heat. When agar-agar has dissolved, add $1\frac{1}{4}$ pints orange juice, mix thoroughly, pour into a bowl or individual glasses and leave to set. Mix 2 mashed bananas with 3 tablespoons cream to a smooth paste. Add 1 teaspoon lemon juice and $1\frac{1}{2}$ oz. sugar. Fold in $\frac{1}{3}$ pint whipped cream and use to garnish the orange mixture.

VEGETABLE COOKERY

In no other field has the old method of cooking been discredited so thoroughly as in the preparation of vegetables. In 1888, the *Basle Cookery Book* recommended the following method:

'What you should know about green vegetables: do not buy your green vegetables more than a day before you want to use them. Boil in salted water until tender. Use plenty of water to preserve the green colour and get rid of the strong taste. Cook over strong heat and cool in plenty of cold water. Green vegetables may also be prepared the night before use and placed in cold water or, where recommended, sprinkled with salt.'

Vitamin-conscious descendants shudder to think that their grandmothers followed these instructions, completely devitalized their vegetables and poured down the sink any vitamins or mineral salts contained in the cooking water. They have learnt to steam vegetables in their own juice or very little water for as short a time as possible and on low heat, and to season with herbs.

It is impossible in this book to list more than a few vegetable recipes, including some for less well-known vegetables, such as artichokes and fennel, and a number of mixed-vegetable dishes as well.

Globe Artichokes *Artischocken*

Artichokes are imported into Switzerland from France, Italy and Spain. Some are now grown in the Tessin. They are gradually beginning to establish themselves, but the sort used for choicer dishes like stuffed artichoke bottoms are still dear.

4 globe artichokes
½ lemon

Cut off stalks immediately below the bottom. Remove tough, small outer leaves and cut off the points of the remaining leaves. Wash thoroughly under running tap, place in salted water, together with ½ lemon, and cook for 40–50 minutes. When the leaves can be pulled out easily, the artichokes are done. Allow to drain, heads downwards. Serve warm or lukewarm with a white sauce, or cold with mayonnaise. Dip each leaf into the sauce, suck off the fleshy part and leave the remains. As a final delicacy, the bottom is eaten with the sauce.

Stuffed Aubergines (Egg Fruit) *Gefüllte Auberginen*

A few years ago, the typically southern aubergine was to be

found only at specialist greengrocers. Today the dark-purple, smooth-skinned vegetable is common at markets and self-service stores in Switzerland and elsewhere. Aubergines may be fried in deep fat, or stuffed with a meat or vegetable filling, or used as a component of mixed-vegetable dishes.

2 large or 4 small aubergines
1 tablespoon oil
8 oz. minced meat or sausage meat
1 chopped onion
1 tablespoon chopped herbs
¾ oz. diced bacon
2 oz. diced bread
1½ oz. butter
2 oz. grated cheese

Halve unpeeled aubergines lengthways, place in frying pan with the oil, cover and cook slowly for 5 minutes. Mix other ingredients for the stuffing (which may be varied, according to taste, with vegetable left-overs, chopped sausages, cold meat, ham or mushrooms) except butter and cheese. Carefully scoop out the aubergines, add scooped-out part to the stuffing and fill aubergine halves. Sprinkle with grated cheese, dot with butter and bake in medium-hot oven (400°F./Gas mark 6) for 20–30 minutes.

Beans *Bohnen*

Try sweating them this way, with little fat and very little water, for not more than 20 minutes, instead of using lots of water.

2¼ lb. well-washed green beans
1 tablespoon chopped onion
1½ oz. butter or fat
parsley
chives
3¾ oz. diced bacon (optional)
salt
pepper
1 pint hot water or vegetable stock
knob of butter (optional)

Heat fat and add onion and, if desired, the bacon. Add well-drained beans and shake saucepan so as to mix them with the fat. Pour in 1 pint hot water or vegetable stock, cover saucepan and leave on mild heat for 15 minutes, occasionally shaking pan. If water is completely absorbed, add a little more. Add salt and pepper and leave for a few minutes more over heat. Serve with parsley, chives and, if liked, a knob of butter.

Chicory *Chicoree*

Not everyone likes the typical, slightly bitter taste of chicory, which is more noticeable in the cooked vegetable than in a raw salad; but others like it particularly.

1¾ lb. chicory
2 oz. butter
grated cheese (optional)

The chicory should be tightly closed. Wash thoroughly, remove lower end and hollow out the remaining stem slightly (the source of the bitter taste). Melt butter in an enamel saucepan and put in the chicory side by side. Sprinkle with little salt and steam without adding any liquid, or with 2-6 fl. oz. beef stock, in covered saucepan for 30 minutes on lowest possible heat. If desired, the chicory may then be sprinkled with grated cheese and baked in the oven for a few minutes.

Corn on the Cob *Maiskolben*

Young corn on the cob has in recent years found favour in Switzerland, as elsewhere.

Per person:

1 cob
butter
salt
pepper

Only young corn is suitable for this dish. Test by scratching one grain with your finger-nail. It should be soft and juicy. Remove green leaves and the silky 'hair' and place cobs in simmering, slightly salted water. Boil for 4 minutes, not longer. The corn becomes harder, not softer, through longer boiling. Lift out and serve with fresh butter, salt and pepper. Each person takes a cob, dips it in butter, sprinkles it with salt and pepper and bites the grains off the cob.

Cos Lettuce with Ham and Mushroom Sauce
Gedämpfte Lattiche mit Schinkenfüllung

The inner leaves of the cos can be used for a salad; and the cos may also be cooked as below, with or without the sauce, baked covered with cheese, or served with fried bacon or with a meat stuffing.

6 medium-sized cos lettuce
1¾ oz. butter or fat
3¾ oz. cooked ham
3¾ oz. mushrooms
1 chopped onion
10 fl. oz. water or meat stock
2½ fl. oz. cream

Remove tough outer leaves and halve the lettuce. The hearts may be removed and used for salad. Wash lettuce thoroughly, cook 5 minutes in boiling salted water, drain. Sweat the chopped onion, chopped mushrooms and chopped ham in butter until tender. Place parboiled cos side by side in fireproof dish, pour over the ham-and-mushroom mixture and the stock, and braise in oven (400°F./Gas mark 6) for 30 minutes. Add cream 5 minutes before end of cooking time.

Baked Fennel *Fenchel*

Fennel possesses an aroma all its own. The tender inner leaves, sprinkled with lemon juice, are excellent raw.

6 medium-sized fennel roots
1 chopped onion
1½ oz. fat or butter
1 pint meat or vegetable stock
2 oz. grated cheese
1 dessertspoon breadcrumbs
1 oz. butter

Remove tough outer leaves and halve fennel roots. Keep back tender inner leaves (and remove hearts if required for salad). Sauté the onion in fat, add fennel roots with the stock and cook slowly until soft. Alternatively, boil in salted water until tender. Place roots, curved side upwards, in fireproof dish, sprinkle with chopped fennel leaves, grated cheese and breadcrumbs, dot a few flakes of butter over the top and bake in oven (400°F./Gas mark 6) for about 30–40 minutes until brown.

Young Peas in the Pod *Kefen*

The tender peapods are delicious but the strings should be removed very carefully. Unfortunately there is as yet no stringless variety.

1¾ lb. peas in the pod
1½ oz. butter or fat
1 teaspoon flour
salt
2 dessertspoons cream
1 chopped onion
good ½ pint meat stock or water
chopped herbs
3¾ oz. diced bacon (optional)

Heat fat and add chopped onion and peapods. Cover saucepan and leave on gentle heat for about 5 minutes. Sprinkle over the flour and gradually add liquid, little more or less according to size of saucepan, but not more than about ⅝ inch. After further 5 minutes, add salt and shake saucepan well. Finally add cream (or half cream, half white wine) and sprinkle with chopped herbs. If bacon is used, fry diced bacon in fat till golden-yellow before adding onion and peapods.

Steamed Leeks *Gedämpftes Lauchgemüse*

2¼ lb. leeks
1 oz. butter
1 teaspoon flour
1 potato (optional)
2-6 fl. oz. water or stock
grated cheese

Clean leeks, cut in finger-long pieces and again wash thoroughly. Fry on all sides in hot butter. Sprinkle with flour, pour in very little water or stock, cover pan and leave to cook on very low heat for 15 minutes. The addition of a grated potato will moderate the strong leek taste, but in this case add little more water. Finally sprinkle over grated cheese.

Mangel Stalks *Krautstiele*

In Switzerland the stalks and veins of large mangel leaves are sold in bunches and used as a vegetable served with a white sauce, with cheese and brown butter, or baked with cheese.

1½ lb. mangel or cabbage stalks
good ¼ pint water
good ¼ pint milk
1 dessertspoon lemon juice
salt
butter
grated cheese
chopped parsley
chopped chives

Remove leaves and fibres and cut stalks into approx. 2–4 inch lengths. Add lemon juice, salt, to the milk and water (or water only) and cook stalks for 15 minutes in the liquid. Drain, sprinkle with grated cheese, add few spoonfuls of brown butter and finally sprinkle with chopped parsley and chives.

Neuchâtel Onion Salad *Neuenburger Zwiebelsalat*

6 large onions	salt
1¾ oz. fat	pepper
1 dessertspoon flour	2 dessertspoons vinegar

Peel onions and cut across into slices approx. ⅜-inch thick. Fry slowly in hot fat until golden, lift out, drain, sprinkle with flour, salt and pepper, place in vinegar and bring once to the boil. Serve lukewarm with potatoes boiled in the jacket.

Waadtland Stuffed Onions

Gefüllte Zwiebeln nach Waadtländer Art

The same stuffing can also be used for potatoes.

8 onions, all same size	salt
1–2 milk rolls	pepper
5 fl. oz. milk	marjoram
2 oz. cooked ham	1 cup beef stock
2 oz. minced meat	2 oz. fat
2 eggs	2 oz. grated cheese
chopped parsley	1 tablespoon breadcrumbs

Grate off the crust of the stale rolls and soak them in warm milk. Squeeze out and combine with minced meat, chopped ham, eggs, herbs and seasoning to a smooth mixture. Peel onions and simmer gently in salted water for 20 minutes. (If potatoes are used, peel and parboil in salted water.) Carefully scoop out a little of the inside of the onions, chop and add to the stuffing. Stuff onions (or potatoes), place side by side in buttered fireproof dish, sprinkle with breadcrumbs and grated cheese and pour over stock. Bake in a medium-hot oven (400°F./Gas mark 6) for 30 minutes.

Chopped Peppers *Peperoni-Haschee*

Red, green and yellow, incredibly decorative, the peppers gleam amid the other vegetables. They are delicious in conjunction with other vegetables, or stuffed with rice, with meat or with pasta. It is important to remove pips carefully and try a piece of each pepper before cooking: occasionally a pepper is so hot as to spoil the whole dish.

4–6 peppers
1 tablespoon oil
1 teaspoon lemon juice
chopped herbs
small clove of garlic (optional)

Rub peppers with a cloth and bake on baking sheet in very hot oven (445°F./Gas mark 8)—better still on a fork at the open fire—for 30 minutes or until the outer skin is burnt black. Remove black tissue-like skin and the pips (it does not matter if a few remain) and chop the peppers. Add oil, lemon juice, herbs and, if desired, finely chopped clove of garlic, and serve with veal chops, or on toast.

Steamed Spinach *Gedämpfter Blatt-Spinat*

People who cook spinach the 'old' way as a purée with white sauce do not know what they are missing. Even that conservative dish can be much improved by the addition, just before serving, of a handful of raw spinach, well washed and chopped and mixed into the purée, but neither its taste nor its nutritional value can stand comparison with steamed whole leaves of spinach.

2¼ lb. young spinach
1 chopped onion
clove of garlic (optional)
1 oz. butter
salt or other seasonings
grated cheese

Lightly cook onion, and, if desired, the garlic, in butter until golden. Wash and drain the spinach, cutting up the big leaves and removing any tough stalks. Add to the onion and steam in a covered saucepan on a low heat for not longer than 5–10 minutes. Do not add any liquid. Season only when spinach is done, then sprinkle with grated cheese and either serve immediately, or place in a hot oven (425°F./Gas mark 7) for 5 minutes or until cheese melts.

Stuffed Tomatoes *Freiburger Tomaten*

4 large or 8 medium-sized tomatoes
3¾ oz. diced Gruyère cheese
3¾ oz. diced potatoes
1 chopped onion
chives
parsley
salt
pepper
1 oz. butter

Halve large tomatoes and scoop out both halves—if medium-sized, cut off a lid at the top and scoop out. Stuff the tomatoes with the ingredients above, dot with butter and bake in hot oven (400°F./Gas mark 6) for 20 minutes.

Sour Turnips *Sauerräben*

In Switzerland turnips are rarely used as a vegetable. In the autumn the children cut holes in hollowed turnips, put in a candle and at night run through the streets with their 'turnip lamps'. For this recipe, the turnips are shredded finely and pickled like sauerkraut, and are frequently served in a mixture of half turnips and half sauerkraut.

***Zucchini* in Batter** *Zucchetti im Ausbackteig*

In recent years these baby marrows have gained popularity in Switzerland. Since they have no strong flavour, they are good in mixed-vegetable dishes, for instance, with tomatoes and peppers, or fried in breadcrumbs or batter, or without any coating, in deep fat.

1 lb. 6 oz. *zucchini*
5 oz. flour
2½ fl. oz. milk
salt
1 egg yolk
1 dessertspoon oil
1 whisked egg white
fat or oil for frying

Young, thin *zucchini* need not be peeled. It is sufficient to rub them in a cloth. Older ones should be peeled. Cut *zucchini* across, or lengthwise, in approx. $\frac{3}{16}$-inch-thick slices. Mix other ingredients for the batter. Dip *zucchini* in the batter and fry in deep fat or oil until golden-brown. Garnish with fried sprigs of parsley. Serve with lemon slices, with mayonnaise or with a well-seasoned tomato sauce.

Peppers and Tomatoes *Peperonata nach Tessiner Art*

Vegetables steamed in their own juice or with very little liquid are especially suitable for combining in dishes of various kinds, like this or the recipes that follow.

1 large onion
2 dessertspoons oil
1 lb. 2 oz. peppers
2¼ lb. tomatoes
salt

Sauté the chopped onion in oil. Cut peppers in strips and remove pips. Add to onions and steam in covered saucepan over low heat for 20 minutes. Then add tomatoes—if desired, skinned and with pips removed. Season with salt, raise heat and cook until there is sufficient liquid to make a sauce.

Southern Mixed Vegetables *Südlandisches Mischgemüse*

1 lb. 2 oz. tomatoes
10 oz. aubergines
10 oz. *zucchini*
2 onions
1 clove of garlic (optional)
chopped fresh or dried herbs (rosemary, marjoram, basil, thyme)
3 tablespoons oil

Peel all vegetables, and where necessary remove pips, and dice. Heat oil in a saucepan, add coarsely chopped onions and gradually the other vegetables, etc. Cover and cook slowly till tender.

Beans and Tomatoes *Bohnen mit Tomaten*

2¼ lb. green beans
1 lb. 2 oz. tomatoes
1 onion
1 dessertspoon oil or fat
salt
parsley
1–2 spoonfuls water or stock (optional)

If the beans are cooked with the tomatoes, no further liquid need be added. Lightly cook onions in fat, add beans and shake saucepan until the beans appear covered with fat. Add sliced or quartered tomatoes, salt, and cook gently in covered saucepan for 20–40 minutes, according to age and variety of beans. From time to time check that liquid is sufficient, if necessary adding 1–2 spoonfuls water or stock. Serve with chopped parsley. (For added flavour, cook 2 peppers with the beans and tomatoes.)

Mixed Vegetables with Chestnuts

Gemüseragout mit Kastanien

1 medium-sized cabbage
1 lb. 2 oz. carrots
1 onion
3¾ oz. diced bacon
1 dessertspoon fat
1 large or 2 small heads of celery
2 leeks
1¾ lb. peeled chestnuts
2½ fl. oz. cream

Fry the bacon in fat until translucent, add chopped onion and then the rest of the vegetables: the cabbage roughly shredded, the celery in strips, the leeks in slices, the carrots in strips or sliced. Finally add peeled chestnuts and little more liquid. Shake well together and cook until tender, shaking repeatedly. Add cream and serve.

APPENDIX I

A LITTLE LIST OF SWISS SAUSAGES

The following list was published by the Swiss Butchers Association. An asterisk indicates that the sausage, or one similar, is generally available outside the country.

Cold Sausages

*Cervela (Klopfer Knackwurst is similar and generally available)
Schützenwurst
Schwartenmagen (made with smoked brawn)
*Streichleberwurst (soft liver sausage)
*Zungenwurst (tongue sausage)

Boiling Sausages

*Blutwurst (black pudding)
*Cervela (see above)
Emmentalerli
*Frankfürterli (Frankfurters)
Grüne Wurst (green sausage)
Knackerli
*Leberwurst (liver sausage)
Schüblig
Schützenwurst
*Schweinswürstli (pork sausage)
*Wienerli (Viennas)
*Zungenwurst (tongue sausage)

Frying Sausages

*Cipolata (Luganerli etc.; some Swiss varieties are made with vegetables)
*Kalbsbratwurst (veal sausage, Extrawurst is similar)
*Schweinsbratwurst (pork sausage)

Uncooked Sausages

Alpenklübler
Bauernschüblig
Landjäger
*Mettwurst
Pantli
*Salametti (Cacciatori is similar)
*Salami
Salsiz

Sausages for Slicing (and Sandwiches)

Balleron
*Bierwurst (beer sausage)
Fleischkäse
Kalbsfleischwurst (veal sausage)
*Lyoner (Extrawurst is similar)
*Mortadella
Presskopf
Presswurst

Western Swiss Specialities

Neuenburger Saucisson (Neuchâtel sausage)
Saucisses au choux (made with cabbage)
Saucisses au foie (made with liver)
Waadtländer Bratwurst (frying sausage)
Waadtländer Saucisson

Tessin Specialities

Coppa
Cottechini
Luganighe
Zamponi

APPENDIX 2
DIFFERENT SWISS BREADS

In German-speaking Switzerland, bread is most generally dark or half-white. It is sold in long or round loaves and known as *Kilobrot* or *Pfundbrot* ('Pfunderli'), according to the quantity.

St Galler Brot is a round, half-white loaf that is common and popular everywhere. *Basler Brot*, *Buurebrot* (literally, peasant bread), and *Bernerbrot* are other well-known varieties.

Vollkornbrot is wholemeal and is far more widespread than ever before; there is hardly a baker today who does not sell various kinds. The best-known varieties are: *Bircherbrot*, *Steinmetzbrot*, *Roggenvollkornbrot* (rye wholemeal bread), *Grahambrot* and *Wallisbrot*.

Pariserbrot or *Parisette* is a long, thin, crisp white bread—what is generally known as 'French bread'.

Modelbrot is baked in a closed mould. It may be white or half-white, oblong or round—'*model*' is a dialect word for a baking tin used in southern Germany and Switzerland. *Toastbrot* is baked in a mould open at the top.

Bürli are made from half-white flour. *Schiltbrot* is similar, but pointed in shape and lighter than Bürli.

The dough for *Weggli* and *Gipfeli* is made with butter and milk. *Pariser Gipfel* are made from a yeast puff paste.

Semmeli are small, crisp, flour-and-water rolls—*Kaisersemmeli*, *Mohnsemmeli* with poppy seeds, and *Salzsemmeli* are a few. *Murren* or *Mutchli* are similar, but larger. *Cornetti* ('little horns') come from the Tessin, like the *Tessiner Brote* which are scored in sections.

Butterwecken, a special Sunday bread, are now of course sold all the week. These big white loaves are made from a milk-egg-and-butter dough of varying richness, brushed with egg yolk and baked golden-brown. The best-known kinds are the *Berner Züpfe*, or plaits (see p. 68). *Züricher Butterwecken* are crescent-shaped and scored on the top; *Basler Ankenwecken* are also curved and scored; in Neuchâtel, the plaited dough is given an oblong form and known as *Taillaules*.

BIBLIOGRAPHY

In compiling this cookery book, I have used many recipes which were given to me orally or in writing, and consulted earlier cookery books, amongst them the following:

Schweizer Küchenspezialitäten. Gute Plättli aus allen Kantonen. Ausgewählt von Helen Guggenbühl (new edition 1950: Schweizerspiegel Verlag, Zürich)

Hundert Küchenspezialitäten aus allen Kantonen (published by Maggis Foodstuffs, Kempttal)

Kochrezepte bündnerischer Frauen (Verlag der Sektion Chur des Schweizer, Gemeinnützigen Frauenvereins)

Le ricette della Nonna. Raccolta di recette ticinesi. Curate da Noride Beretta-Verenna e da Giovanna Sciaroni-Moretti (Tipografia Pax, Locarno-Muralto)

150 *x Kartoffeln. Rezepte bearbeitet von Rosa Graf-Wüest* (Selbstverlag der Propagandazentrale für Erzeugnisse der Schweiz, Landwirtschaft Zürich: 7th edition, 1942)

Gaumenfreuden mit Käse (published by Schweiz. Käseunion A.G., Bern)

Kochbuch by Elisabeth Fülscher (7th edition, 1960: published by Elisabeth Fülscher, Zürich)

INDEX OF ENGLISH NAMES

(*For* Index of Swiss Names *see* p. 145)

Almond
  Biscuits, 101
  Pastry, Glarn Jam and, 97
Aniseed Biscuits, 101
Apple
  Batter, Fried, 74
  Juice, 116
  Pancakes, Bernese, 74
  Potato and Bacon Stew, 55
  Purée, 124
  Rolls, 81
  Tart, 77
Apples
  Dried, with Bacon and Potatoes, 35
  Fried, 70
Apricot Tart, 78
Artichokes, Globe, 125
Aubergines, Stuffed, 125

Bacon
  with Dried Apples and Potatoes, 35
  Squares, Onion and, 81
  Stew
    Apple, Potato and, 55
    with Young Peas, 36
  Tart, 76
Banana Cream, Orange and, 124
Barley Soup, Engadine, 4
Batter
  Basic Pancake, 72
  Fried Apple, 74
  Rabbit Baked in, 43
  Zucchini in, 132
Bean
  and Mutton Stew, Swiss, 36
  and Potato Purée, 57
Beans, 126
  and Tomatoes, 133
Beef
  Braised, 39
  Roast Fillet of, 39
  Stew, 40
Beetroot Salad, 119
Bernese Board, 34
Berry Juice, 117
Biberli, 108
Bircher Muesli: *see* Muesli
Biscuits, 100–109
  Almond, 101
  Aniseed, 101
  Cinnamon, 103
    Honey (Rings), 108
  'Dead Men's Bones', 103
  Dripping, 104
  Hazelnut, 101
  Honey, 105
  Macaroons, 105
  Marzipan, Zürich, 106
  Milanese, 102
  Nut and Honey, 107
  Spagnoletti, 102
  Spicy Sugar Rusks, 104
Bonbons, Cream, 109
Bread, 68
  -and-Cheese
    Fritters, 70
    Pudding, 16
  kinds of, 19
  Pear, 98
  Soup, 3
  ways with Stale, 69
  Yeast Plait, 68
Butter Dishes, 68

Cabbage
  with Mutton, Braised, 34
  and Rice, 64
  Soup, 7
Cake
  Carrot, 9
  Cheese, 17
    Appenzell, 18
  Cherry, 95
    Chocolate, 96
  Easter, 78

Cake (Cont.)
Flat
Neuchâtel, 97
Waadtland, 97
Fried Kranz Ring, 91
Nut, Engadine, 93
Pear Bread, 98
Polenta, 64
Tin, 70
Cakes, 87
Cheese
Doughnuts, 90
Tarts, 18
Egg, 89
Fried, 87–92
Spiced, 88
Funnel, 91
Gingerbread Fingers, 73
Pear Rolls, 99
Sage, 87
Schenkeli, 90
Semolina, with Cheese Filling, 18
Carrot Cake, 94
Cauliflower with Mayonnaise, 120
Celery Salad, 119
Cereals, 60
and Fruit, 124
Cheese, 10–22
-baked Potatoes, 54
Balls, 16
Cake, 17
Appenzell, 18
Doughnuts, 90
Fried, 14
Fritters, 19
Basle, 19
Bern, 20
Emmenthal, 20
St Gallen, 20
Waadtland, 19
Kebabs, 21
Pudding, Bread-and-, 16
'Quarrels', 21
Salad, 22
Cheese (Cont.)
Soup, 11
Bündner, 12
Urner, 11
Steak, 15
Tart(s), 18
Cherry
Cake, 95
Chocolate, 96
Pancakes, 74
Tart, 78
Chestnuts
Mixed Vegetables with, 134
Vermicelles, with cream, 84
Chicken, Roast, with Onions and Mushrooms, 46
Chicory, 127
Salad, 118
Cholermues, 73
Cinnamon
Biscuits, 103
Honey Rings, 108
Corn on the Cob, 127
Cos Lettuce
with Ham and Mushroom Sauce, 127
Salad, 118
Country Soup, 6
Cream
Bonbons, 109
Orange and Banana, 124
Peach, 124
Tart, 77
Vermicelles with, 84

'Dead Men's Bones', 103
Desserts, 83
Doughnuts, Cheese, 90
Drinks, 110
Dripping Biscuits, 104
Dumplings, 61
Amplis, 5
Liver, 62
Potato, 56
Small, 56
Semolina Balls, 67

Easter Cake, 78
Egg
-ball, Fried, 88
Cakes, 89
Fruit: *see* Aubergines, 125
-and-Milk Dishes, 69 *et seq.*
See also Omelettes, Pancakes
Elderberry Purée, Toggenburg, 86
Endive Salad, 118

Fennel
Baked, 128
Salad, 118
Fenz, 71
Fish, 23—31
with Brown Sauce, 28
Mixed Fried, 29
Perch
with Almonds, 27
à la Meunière (without almonds), 27
Pickled, 30
Pike, 24
Larded, 26
in Tomato Sauce, 30
Rötel with Wine Sauce, 25
Salmon, Fried, 25
Trout in Geneva Sauce, 29
Whitefish, 24
Baked, 26
with Herb Sauce, 28
with almonds, 27
à la Meunière (without almonds), 27
Flat Cake
Neuchâtel, 97
Waadtland, 97
Flour Soup, Basle, 2
Fondue, 12
Bourguignonne, 37
Chinoise, 38
Geneva, 13
Neuchâtel, 12
Waadtland, 13
Fonduta, 14
Frankfurter Rolls, 80
Fritters
Bread-and-cheese, 70
Cheese, 19
See also Batter, Pancakes
Fruit
Cereals and, 124
Dishes, 123
Juices, 116
and Milk Pudding, 86
Yoghurt and, 123
Funnel Cakes, 91

Gingerbread Fingers, 73

Ham Croissants, 81
Hazelnut Biscuits, 101
Health Cookery, Modern, 114
Heart, Stuffed Calf's, 46
Hirsotto: *see* Millet, Fried
Honey Biscuits, 105
Nut and, 107
Horseradish Salad, Radish and, 119

Jam and Almond Pastry, Glarn, 97
Juices, Fruit and Vegetable, 116

Kohlrabi Salad, 119
Kranz Ring, Fried, 91

Leek(s)
Salad, 119
and Sausage Stew, 50
Steamed, 129
Lettuce
with Ham and Mushroom Sauce, Cos, 127
Salad
Cos, 118
-leaf, 118
Soup, Stuffed, 3
Liver
Diced, 42
Dumplings, 62
Patties, Neuchâtel, 80

Liver (Cont.)
on Skewers, 41

Macaroons, 105
Maize
Fried, 65
Soup, 3
Mangel Stalks, 129
Marrow Soup, Vegetable, 8
Marrows, Baby: *see Zucchini*
Marzipan Biscuits, Zürich, 106
Meat, 32–47
Balls, 50
Pasty, 43
and Tomato Pie, Potato, 58
See also Beef, Mutton, Pork, Sausages, Veal
Meringue Rings, 84
Milanese Biscuits, 102
Milk
Dishes, 71
Pudding, 71
Fruit and, 86
Millet, Fried, 66
Minestrone, 7
Muesli, 121
Original, 122
Mutton
Braised Cabbage with, 34
Leg of, Braised, 35
Stew, Swiss Bean and, 36

Nut
Cake, Engadine, 93
and Honey Biscuits, 107

Omelette, Jura, 73
Omelettes, 72
Onion
and Bacon Squares, 81
Salad, Neuchâtel, 130
Tart, 76
Onions
Sausage Meat with, 51
Waadtland Stuffed, 130
Orange and Banana Cream, 124
Oranges, Strawberries and, 123
Pancake
Batter, Basic, 72
Rolls, 73
Soup, 3
Pancakes, 72
Bernese Apple, 74
Cherry, 74
Cholermues, 73
Pasta, 60
Potatoes and, 62
Pasties, 79
Pastry
Glarn Jam and Almond, 97
Tart, 76
Pasty, Meat, 43
Pea Soup with Gnagi, 4
Peach Cream, 124
Pear
Bread, 98
Rolls, 99
Peas
Bacon Stew with Young, 36
in the Pod, Young, 128
Peppers
Chopped, 131
and Tomatoes, 133
Perch
with Almonds, 27
à la Meunière, 27
Pike
Larded, 26
in Tomato Sauce, 30
Plum Tart, 78
Polenta, 64
Cake, 100
Fried or Baked, 65
Poltö, 71
Poor Man's Trout, 48
Pork
Sausages cooked in Wine, 50
Stew, 37
Pot-au-feu, 33
Pot Soup with Amplis, 5
Potato
and Bacon Stew, Apple, 55

Potato (Cont.)
Crumbs, Sauté, 55
Meat and Tomato Pie, 58
-Pitte, 58
Purée,
Baked, 57
Bean and, 57
Potatoes, 52–59
Bacon with Dried Apples and, 35
in Brown Sauce, 54
Cheese-baked, 54
Dumplings, 56
Small, 56
Fribourg Fried, 53
and Pasta, 62
Swiss Fried, 52
Pudding
Bread-and-Cheese, 16
with Grated Cheese, 16
with Sliced Cheese, 16
Milk, 71
Fruit and, 86
Savoury, 66

Rabbit
Baked in Batter, 43
Stuffed, 42
Raclette: *see* Cheese, Fried
Radish and Horseradish Salad, 119
Ramequin: *see* Bread-and-Cheese Pudding
Rhubarb Tart, 78
Rice, 60
Cabbage and, 64
Risotto, 63
Rösti: *see* Potatoes, Swiss Fried
Rötel with Wine Sauce, 25

Sage Cakes, 87
Salad Dressings, 117
Salads, 117–120
Beetroot, 119
Celery, 119
Cheese, 22
Chicory, 118
Salads (Cont.)
Cos Lettuce, 118
Endive, 118
Fennel, 118
Horseradish, Radish and, 119
Kohlrabi, 119
Leek, 119
Lettuce-leaf, 118
Mixed, 120
Onion, Neuchâtel, 130
Radish and Horseradish, 119
Sauerkraut, 119
Sausage, 49
Spinach, 118
Traditional Mixed, 117
Salmon, Fried, 25
Sandwiches, Open, 121
Sauerkraut
Juice, 117
Salad, 119
Sausage
Grilled, 49
Meat with Onions, 51
Rolls, 79
Salad, 49
Stew, Leek and, 50
Sausages, 48–51
List of, 135
with Onion Sauce, 49
Poor Man's Trout, 48
Pork, cooked in Wine, 50
on Skewers, 49
Znüni, 48
Schenkeli, 90
Semolina
Balls, 67
Cakes with Cheese Filling, 18
Soups, 1–9
Barley, Engadine, 4
Bread, 3
Cabbage, 7
Cheese
Bündner, 12
Urner, 11
Country, 6
Flour, Basle, 2

Soups (Cont.)
  Lettuce, Stuffed, 3
  Maize, 3
  Minestrone, 7
  Pancake, 3
  Pea, with Gnagi, 4
  Pot, with Amplis, 5
  Spinach, 5
  Tripe, 8
  Vegetable Marrow, 8
Spagnoletti, 102
Spiced Cakes, Fried, 88
Spicy Sugar Rusks, 104
Spinach
  Dumplings, 61
  Rolls, 62
  Salad, 118
  Soup, 5
  Steamed, 131
  Tart, 77
Steak, Cheese, 15
Stews
  Apple, Potato and Bacon, 55
  Bacon with Dried Apples and Potatoes, 35
  Bacon, with Young Peas, 36
  Bean and Mutton, Swiss, 36
  Beef, 40
  Leek and Sausage, 50
  Pork, 37
  Pot-au-feu: see Stockpot
  Stockpot, 33
  Veal, Brown, 40
Strawberries and Oranges, 123
Sweets: *see* Desserts

Tart
  Dough (Yeast), 76
  Pastry, 76
Tart(s), 75–79
  Apple, 77
  Apricot, 78
  Bacon, 76
  Cheese, 18
  Cherry, 78
  Cream, 77
  Onion, 76
Tart(s) (Cont.)
  Plum, 78
  Rhubarb, 78
  Spinach, 77
Tin Cake, 70
Tomato
  Juice, 116
  Pie, Potato, Meat and, 58
Tomatoes
  Beans and, 133
  Peppers and, 133
  Stuffed, 132
Tripe
  Soup, 8
  with Tomato Sauce, 44
Trout in Geneva Sauce, 29
Turnips, Sour, 132

Veal
  Diced, 41
  Schnitzel
    Cordon Bleu, 45
    Emmenthal, 45
  Stew, Brown, 40
Vegetable
  Cookery, 124
  Juices, 116
Vegetables
  Mixed
    with Chestnuts, 134
    Southern, 133
  Raw, Presenting, 120
Vermicelles with Cream, 84

Wähen: *see* Tarts
Whitefish
  with Almonds, 27
  Baked, 26
  with Herb Sauce, 28
  à la Meunière, 27

Yeast
  Dough, 76
  Plait, 68
Yoghurt and Fruit, 123

Zabaione, 85
Znüni, 48
Zucchini in Batter, 132

INDEX OF SWISS NAMES

(*For* English Index *see* p. 139)

Adrio, 51
Agoni in Carpione, 30
Amaretti, 105
Apfelrösti, 70
Apfelsaft, 116
Apfelwähe, 77
Apfelweggen, 81
Appenzeller Käsfladen, 18
Aprikosenwähe, 78
Artischocken, 125
Auberginen (Eierfrüchte), 125

Bacheschnitte, 73
Badener Kräbeli, 101
Basler Leckerli, 105
Basler Mehlsuppe, 2
Basler Pfnutli, 74
Beefsteak au fromage, 15
Beerensaft, 117
Berner Apfel-Omelette, 74
Berner Platte, 34
Berner Strübli, 91
Biberli, 108
Birchermüesli, 122
Birnbrot, 98
Birnwecken, 99
Blechkuchen nach Neuenburger Art, 97
Blechkuchen nach Waatländer Art, 97
Blumenkohl mit Mayonnaise, 120
Bohnen, 126
Bohnen mit Tomaten, 133
Bohnentopf, Innerschweizer, 36
Böllewegge, 81
Brätkügeli, 50
Bratwürste mit Zwiebelsauce, 49
Bratwurst, Waadtländer, 50
Brot, Allerlei aus altbackenem, 69
Brunsli, 101
Brunsli mit Haselnüssen, 101
Brunsli mit Mandeln, 101
Bündner Käsesuppe, 12
Busecca (Kuttelsuppe), 8

Cervela, 49
Chäs-Happech, 16
Chicoree, 127
Chicoree, grüner, 118
Chicoreesalat, 118
Chifelstunggis, 36
Cholermues, 73
Chriesi-Omelette, 74
Conterser Bock, 88
Creme aus rohen Äpfeln, 124

Dünkli-Suppe, 3

Egli oder Felchen à la meunière, 27
Egli oder Felchen mit Mandeln, 27
Eierkutteln, 73
Eieröhrli, 89
Emmentaler Schnitzel, 45
Engadiner Gerstensuppe, 4
Engadiner Nusstorte, 93
Erbssuppe mit Gnagi, 4
Erdbeeren mit Orangen, 123

Felchen; 24 *and see* Egli,
Felchen im eigenen Saft mit Kräutersauce, 28
Fenchel, 128
Fenchelsalat, 118
Fenz, 71
Fettgebackenes, 87

Feula-Pitte, 104
Fische nach Walchwiler Art, 28
Flädli-Suppe, 3
Flockenspeisen, 124
Fondue, 12
Fondue Bourguignonne, 37
Fondue Chinoise, 38
Fondue, Genfer, 13
Fondue, Neuenburger, 12
Fondue, Waadtländer, 13
Fonduta, 14
Forellen mit Genfer Sauce, 29
Freiburger Kartoffeln, 53
Freiburger Tomaten, 132
Friture du lac, 29
Frucht- und Gemüsesäfte, 116
Fruchtspeisen, 123

Gemüseragout mit Kastanien, 134
Genfer Fondue, 13
Gitzi, gefülltes, 42
Gitziprägel, 43
Glarner Pastete, 97
Gnagi; *see* Erbssuppe, 4
Griessküchlein mit Käse, 18
Griess-Pfluten, 67
Guetzli, 100
Güggeli, 46

Hafensuppe mit Amplis, 5
Hecht, gespickter, nach Basler Art, 26
Hecht in Tomatensauce nach Tessiner Art, 30
Hefeteig, 76
Heidelbeerbrei, 86
Hirse, 67
Hirsotto, 66
Holder-Mus, Toggenburger, 86
Honigleckerli, 107

Jura-Omelette, 73

Kalbfleisch, geschnetzeltes, 41
Kalbsherz, gefülltes, 46
Kalbsschnitzel Cordon bleu, 45
Kartoffel- und Bohnenpüree, 57
Kartoffeln, Freiburger, 53
Kartoffeln und Teigwaren, 62
Kartoffeln, Tessiner, 54
Kartoffelpfluten, 56
Kartoffel-Pitte, 58
Kartoffelspätzli, 61
Kartoffel-Tomaten Torte, 58
Käsegezänke, 21
Käsepastetchen, 18
Käsesalat, 22
Käseschnitten, 19
Käseschnitten Basler Art, 19
Käseschnitten Berner Art, 20
Käseschnitten Emmentaler Art, 20
Käseschnitten St Galler Art, 20
Käseschnitten Waadtländer Art, 19
Käsespiesschen mit Schachtelkäse, 21
Käsesuppe, Bündner, 12
Käsesuppe, Urner, 11
Käsewähe, 17
Käsfladen, Appenzeller, 18
Kefen (Zuckerschoten), 128
Kirschentorte mit Schokolade, 96
Kirschenwähe, 78
Kirschtorte, Zuger, 95
Knöpfli, 61
Kohlrabi als Rohsalat, 119
Kohlsuppe, 7
Kopfsalatsuppe, 3
Kräbeli, Badener, 101
Kranz, gebackener, 91
Krautkapaunen, 62
Krautstiele, 129
Kügelipastete, 43
Kürbissuppe, 8
Kutteln nach Schaffhauser Art, 44
Kuttelsuppe, 8

Lachs nach Basler Art, 25
Lattich, 127
Lattichsalat, 118
Lauchgemüse, 129
Lauchgemüse mit Wurst, 50
Lauchsalat, 119
Leber, geschnetzelte, 42
Leber-Spätzli, 62
Leberspiesschen, 41
Lummelbraten, 39

Mailänderli, 102
Maiskolben, 127
Maissuppe, 3
Maluns, 55
Marzipanleckerli, Zürcher, 106
Matafan, 70
Minestrone, 7
Mischsalate, 120
Mischgemüse, 133
Mistchratzerli, 46

Neuenburger Leberpastetchen, 80
Neuenburger Zwiebelsalat, 130
Nidelwähe, 77
Nidelzeltli, 109
Nusstorte, Engadiner, 93

Ofenguck, 57
Ofentori, 57
Omeletten, 72
Orangencreme mit Bananenrahm, 124
Osterfladen, 78
Oster-Gitzi, gefülltes, 42

Pastete, Glarner, 97
Patlaunas, 88
Peperoni (Pfefferschoten), 131
Peperonata nach Tessiner Art, 133
Pfirsichcreme, rohe, 124
Pizokel, 56
Plain in pigna, 66
Plattenmüesli, 71
Polenta, 64
Polenta-Kuchen, 100
Polenta-Schnitten, aufgebackene, 65
Poltö, 71
Pot-au-feu, 33

Raclette, 14
Radieschen- und Rettichsalat, 119
Ramequin, 16
Ramequin mit geriebenem Käse, 16
Ramequin mit Käsescheiben, 16
Randen (Rote Rüben) als Rohsalat, 119
Rhabarberwähe, 78
Rindsvoressen, 40
Risotto, 63
Rohe Pfirsichcreme, 124
Rohgemüseplatte, 120
Rohkost-Sandwiches, 121
Rösti, 53
Rötel nach Zuger Art, 25
Rüeblitorte, 94

Salate und Rohgemüse, 120
Salatsaucen, 117
Salat von verschiedenen Kräutern, 117
Salbeiküchlein, 87
Sauce, Genfer, 29
Saucen-Gummeli, 54
Sauerkrautsaft, 117
Sauerkrautsalat, 119
Sauerräben, 132
Schaffhauser Schübling-Weggen, 80
Schafstotzen im Becki, 35
Schenkeli, 90
Schinkenfüllung, 127
Schinkengipfeli, 81
Schnittsalat, 118
Schnitz und Kartoffeln, 35
Schnitzel, Emmentaler, 45
Schübling-Weggen, 80

Sellerie, roher, als Salat, 119
's Köch, 55
Spagnoletti, 102
Spätzli, 61, 62
Speckwähe, 76
Spinat, 131
Spinatsalat, 118
Spinat-Spätzli, 61
Spinatsuppe, 5
Spinatwähe, 77
Stufato alla Chiessese, 39
Stunggis, 37

Teigwaren, 61
Tessiner Kartoffeln, 54
Toggenburger Holder-Mus, 86
Tomaten, Freiburger, 132
Tomaten, gefüllte, 120
Tomatensaft, 116
Totenbeinli, 103
Triätschnitten, 104
Türkenribel, 65

Urner Häfelikabis, 34
Urner Käsesuppe, 11
Urner Kraut mit Reis, 64

Vacherin, 84
Vermicelles mit Schlagrahm, 84
Vogelheu, 70
Voressen, 40

Waadtländer Bratwurst, 50
Waadtländer Fondue, 13
Wähen, 75
Wähenteig, 76
Willisauer Ringli, 108
Wurstweggen, 79

Yoghurt-Fruchtspeise, 123

Zabaione, 85
Zeltli, 100
Ziegerkrapfen, 90
Zimt-Pitte, 103
Znüni, 48
Zucchetti, 132
Zuger Ballen, 26
Zuger Kirschtorte, 95
Züpfe (Hefezopf), 68
Zuppa del paes, 6
Zürcher Marzipanleckerli, 106
Züri-Chrebs, 48
Zwetschenwähe, 78
Zwiebeln, gefüllte, nach Waadtländer Art, 130
Zwiebelsalat, Neuenburger, 130
Zwiebelwähe, 76